On the Importance of Small Farms in Michigan

Public Comments on Right to Farm and the 2014 Site Selection GAAMP

Edited by Wendy Lockwood Banka

City Rooster Press
ANN ARBOR, MI

City Rooster Press
3291 Rosedale
Ann Arbor, Michigan 48108

ON THE IMPORTANCE OF SMALL FARMS IN MICHIGAN
Public Comments on Right to Farm and the 2014 Site Selection
GAAMP/ Wendy Lockwood Banka — 1st ed.

ISBN 978-0-9862821-0-2

"The difficulty of the issue, in terms of legal versus non-legal uses, is that the RTF Act itself does not place a restriction in any way on land use or land zoning. It has been very clear from the beginning the RTF Act applies across the entire state."

Jim Johnson, Director, Environmental Stewardship Division, MDARD
Michigan Commission of Agriculture and Rural Development Minutes
December 14, 2011

CONTENTS

PREFACE

This is a book of excerpts from public comments made by Michigan citizens in early 2014, on changes to an obscure state regulatory document called the Site Selection GAAMP. That is one way of looking at it. It might more accurately be described as a book of excerpts from public comments that Michigan citizens made, on why issues of farm and food are so important in 2014. Either way, a bit of background on the GAAMPS and their relationship to Right to Farm will help put the public comments in context, and may help explain why a thousand or more Michigan citizens took the time to speak so passionately and so eloquently to our state government about agricultural policy in 2014.

The story really begins in the early 1980's when all states passed Right to Farm (RTF) laws, which were originally designed to protect farmers from the kind of nuisance lawsuits that can arise when people unaccustomed to farming move out of cities and into rural areas. The intent of the law shifted, however, at least in Michigan, as subsequent amendments brought industrial agricultural practices under the clear protection of Right to Farm. Indeed, one could argue that after amendments to Michigan's 1981 RTF law were passed in 1987, 1995, and 1999, the Right to Farm Act became the cornerstone of a legal and policy infrastructure largely designed to support and enable corporate agriculture in Michigan.

The 1999 amendment is especially noteworthy, since it added language to prohibit local regulations such as ordinances or zoning from impeding farm operations that meet the requirements of the RTFA; as a result of this amendment, Michigan's Right to Farm Act came to be known as the strongest in the nation. Less widely appreciated is the fact that language has also been introduced into other Michigan laws to provide additional protections to farmers who meet RTF criteria; in March 1991, for example, Director of the Michigan Department of Agriculture Bill Schuette stated that farmers meeting Right to Farm guidelines were also exempt from Air Quality Permit requirements, Water Quality Permit requirements, and liability under the 1990 Polluter's Pay Law. Since 1999, then, Michigan's Right to Farm Act itself has protected RTF-compliant farmers against nuisance lawsuits and local regulations, while other Michigan laws have protected RTF-compliant farmers from state-level environmental laws.

Farmers wishing to earn the protections of the Right to Farm Act are required to meet two conditions laid out in the Act: first, the farm operation must be commercial, and second, it must adhere to the Generally Accepted Agricultural and Management Practices, or GAAMPs. The definition of "commercial" is easily met, since it has been interpreted by the courts to mean any level of sales, or even intent to sell. The second requirement also tends to be easily met, since the RTFA gave the Commission of Agriculture the authority to define "generally accepted" agricultural management practices rather than "best" management practices. This loose definition provided the Commissioners with considerable leeway, with the result that the GAAMPs have largely been written by farmers for farmers, with a goal of protecting commercial farm operations from nuisance lawsuits from neighbors, regulations from local governments, and environmental laws from the state government.

Of course not all farms have equal requirements for the different protections that exist under Michigan's Right to Farm Act. For example, while traditional farms in Michigan may have benefited from the nuisance protection of the original 1981 RTFA, those farms had little need for the protection from local regulation and environmental laws that came later, since traditional farms were accepted as the norm in rural townships, and because traditional farms cause little environmental harm. In contrast, industrial agriculture could not have easily survived in Michigan if it had not been protected from nuisance lawsuits, local regulations, and environmental laws. On balance, then, the RTF amendments in 1987, 1995, and 1999 increasingly enabled corporate agriculture to dominate food production in Michigan, at the expense of traditional farmers and eaters alike.

Indeed, the satisfaction of Michigan citizens with their food choices has withered to the point that even citizens in urban areas and with small acreage in rural areas are increasingly in search of ways to produce their own food, be it garden, goat, bee, or chicken. Many citizens have discovered that while it is relatively easy to do the work of producing some of their own food, it is difficult or impossible to traverse the strict local regulations in Michigan that prohibit agricultural activity. Very few cities in Michigan allow for the growing of any livestock, for example, and even the regulations around gardens are highly restrictive in many urban areas. Meanwhile, many rural townships have been zoned residential for tax purposes, and with the term "residential" came many of the same kinds of zoning restrictions that were previously developed for urban areas. Thus although a great number of Michigan residents are interested in engaging in agriculture, local regulations have not kept pace, and in most places tightly restrict or outright prohibit the growing of food.

Fortunately, in the fifteen years since the passage of the 1999 RTF amendment, a few small farmers recognized that they were as eligible for Right to Farm protection as any other farmer in Michigan, because the law makes no requirements based on size or place, and instead only requires that the operation be commercial and that it follow applicable GAAMPs. Some small farmers in residentially zoned areas had to go to court to prove this, but they did, and repeatedly prevailed at the Appeals Court level. In 2004 for example, Bill Schuette and two other Appeals Court judges interpreted the Right to Farm Act after 1999 to mean that

> … farming operations that conform to GAAMPs are not public nuisances, even when they change size, ownership, or the type of product produced. Hence, because an ordinance provision that only permits single family dwellings, playgrounds, and parks would prohibit farming operations, the ordinance provision conflicts with the RTFA and is unenforceable.[1]

Thus there was a brief interval between 1999 and 2011 when the way forward for agriculture seemed clear for the majority of the state that lives in residentially zoned areas – both rural and urban – and it was called Right to Farm.

In 2011, however, the Michigan Department of Agriculture (MDA) came under the leadership of a new administration and was renamed the Michigan Department of Agriculture and Rural Development (MDARD). This change in department name foreshadowed a real shift in department policy to focus only on agriculture in areas that are rural and zoned for agriculture – despite the fact that the courts had already

---

1 Village of Rothbury v Double JJ Resort Ranch, Inc. State of Michigan Court of Appeals, 2004. Decided by Judges Whitbeck, Owens, and Schuette.

concluded that Right to Farm protects all farms in Michigan, regardless of size or place. This conflict between what the law required and what the agency desired created a conundrum for MDARD. The appropriate mechanism to resolve it would have been to convince the legislature to again amend the Right to Farm Act to restrict its provisions.

Indeed, in 2011 state Senators Virgil Smith and Joe Hune prepared just such a bill to exempt the city of Detroit from Right to Farm protection[2], and planned to introduce it on November 11, 2011[3]. That bill was never introduced, however, for reasons that Senator Smith explained on his website:

> I drafted a bill that would exempt Detroit from the Right to Farm Act and State Senator Joe Hune, who is a Republican, the Chair of the Senate Agriculture Committee, and a farmer, cosponsored my bill. Having a Republican cosponsor this bill is a major accomplishment and has drawn the attention of the powerful farming lobby in Michigan.
>
> Before I introduced my bill which would allow Detroit to control agricultural development in the city, the Michigan Department of Agriculture asked me to wait so they could better explain what they are doing on this issue. On December 14, 2011 the Department will hold a meeting that will allow municipalities with a population of 50,000 or more the ability to regulate farming activity. I hope that this administrative fix will solve our problems and allow urban farming to legally sprout throughout our great cities in Michigan. I have agreed to wait on introducing my bill until after the Dec. 14 meeting to determine whether the administrative fix by the Department sufficiently allows municipalities to regulate urban farming.[4]

Thus MDARD convinced Senators Smith and Hune to refrain from introducing their bill to restrict Right to Farm protections to the legislature,

---

2 Bill would create Right to Farm Act exemption for Detroit. Dawson Bell, Detroit Free Press, November 28, 2011.

3 State Senator looks to amend Michigan Right to Farm Act, let Detroit regulate urban farming. Jonathon Oosting, mLive, November 29, 2011.

4 http://www.virgilksmith.com/urban-farming/

and to instead allow MDARD to use the GAAMPs as a vehicle to deny legal, legislatively enacted Right to Farm protection to specific subsets of Michigan citizens. At this point the issue grew from a policy question of who should be protected by Right to Farm, to a second, legal question of whether a state agency such as MDARD has the authority to deny Michigan citizens their legal rights as enacted by the state legislature.

This tactic was formally deployed just a few weeks later in December of 2011, when the Michigan Commission of Agriculture approved changes to the 2012 GAAMPs Preface to state that each of the GAAMPs "does not apply" in cities of over 100,000 residents[5]. In 2011, 1.5 million Michigan citizens lived in the seven cities with over 100,000 residents, and ostensibly lost their legal Right to Farm protection because of this change to the language of the GAAMPs, and the vote of five appointed members of the Michigan Commission of Agriculture and Rural Development. In 2011 Bill Schuette was the attorney general, and his office advised the commissioners that they had been

"...working with the department on this issue to meet the policy goals while staying within the confines of the Right to Farm Act. The language proposed would exempt the City of Detroit and other municipalities of 100,000 or more in population from the GAAMPs. It does not, nor does the Commission have the authority, to exempt them from the Right to Farm Act which applies more broadly as a statute. The Attorney General's Office believes what has been proposed is within the confines of the Right to Farm Act and does accomplish the goals being sought."[6]

This statement ignores the public record which clearly shows that the intent of the GAAMPs changes was to deny Right to Farm protection, however, and also ignores the 1:1 relationship between the GAAMPs and Right to Farm that makes this tactic possible: since Right to Farm protection *requires* compliance with the GAAMPs, any change to the GAAMPs that are impossible to meet does effectively deny Right to Farm protection to affected citizens. Public documents record that the City of Detroit had little confidence that this "administrative solution" could

5 Dec. 14, 2011 Minutes of the Michigan Commission of Agriculture and Rural Development.
6 Ibid.

withstand a court challenge[7]. And on February 21, 2012 Senators Smith and Hune requested a formal opinion on the question from Attorney General Bill Schuette[8], but that opinion was never written.

By mid-2012 small farmers began to understand what had happened, and were paying attention when MDARD next proposed changes to the 2013 Site Selection GAAMP, which would have similarly denied Right to Farm protection to all citizens living in residentially zoned areas. Based on USDA numbers it was estimated that about 8 million Michigan citizens or 80 percent of the population lives in these areas, and would be affected by the change. In 2012 small farmers from urban and rural areas argued to the Commission of Agriculture that the 1999 RTF amendment specifically precludes local regulations from impinging on RTF protections for all farmers in the state, regardless of the size or place of the farm, and that the Commission did not have the authority to deny small farmers their legal rights. This effort was successful, as the Commission of Agriculture voted in December of 2012 to send the proposed changes back to the GAAMP Committee for further review[9]. No further changes to the GAAMPs were formally proposed to the Commission in all of 2013.

On January 6, 2014, however, MDARD announced a two-week public comment period on proposed changes to the 2014 Site Selection GAAMP, which again attempted to add language to make it impossible to meet GAAMPs requirements for those living in residentially zoned areas. During the formal public comment period between January 6th and January 22nd , MDARD received responses from 721 people, with 684 of those comments expressing opposition to the proposed changes. In the following weeks MDARD received hundreds more, virtually all of which were also opposed to the proposed changes.

What you now hold in your hands are 121 of the thousand or more public comments received by MDARD opposing changes to the 2014 GAAMPS, that were designed to deny legal Right to Farm protection to

---

7 March 29, 2012 Detroit City Planning Commission Minutes

8 http://sustainablefarmpolicy.org/the-city/

9 Dec. 12, 2012 Minutes of the Michigan Commission of Agriculture and Rural Development

the majority of Michigan citizens who live in residentially zoned areas, without a vote of the legislature.

I decided to publish these public comments because even after working on this issue for several years I was stunned not only by the number of people who wrote to oppose the proposed changes, but also by what they said. I expected the kinds of comments that described the history and the legal implications of the proposed changes. I also expected the thoughtful and informed comments from small farmers who had fought and won Right to Farm cases, and also from those who had fought and lost. But I was unprepared for the letters from small farmers in Michigan who are passionate about keeping livestock because they believe it is an essential component of teaching compassion and responsibility to their children. I also didn't expect the letters that tell the role that urban agriculture is already playing in revitalizing Detroit and other cities, or the letters that told how Right to Farm allowed them to keep animals and feed their families during these very difficult economic times. And I surely did not expect that the dominant over-riding theme across a thousand letters would be that our food system is broken, and is burdening us with a polluted environment and poor health that is already visible in ourselves and in our children.

In the end, I published these public comments because I think that collectively they convey the myriad reasons that small farms matter in 2014, and I want them to continue to be heard as we work toward agricultural policies in Michigan that are broadly acceptable to the people who live here.

Most of the comments that appear here were sent to MDARD via email during the formal public comment period between January 6th and January 22nd, 2014, but some were received by letter, or by video, or during the public input meeting on January 22nd. Other comments that appear here were received by MDARD from January 22nd through March 31st, 2014, and were obtained under the Freedom of Information Act. In addition to the 121 comments published here, nearly 900 additional messages were received by MDARD between January and March 2014, and tell very similar stories to the ones you read here.

A few of the comments are presented exactly as written, but most are excerpts. Typos have been corrected, and on occasion a few words have been deleted simply to make a comment fit on a page.

All are presented with permission of the author.

Wendy Lockwood Banka
December 2, 2014
Ann Arbor

On the Importance of Small Farms in Michigan

Public Comments on Right to Farm and the 2014 Site Selection GAAMP

{1}

I have owned and operated a horse farm on 15 acres of land for 25 years. I am in an agricultural zoned area. There are houses going in around me. I don't know if there are any subdivisions planned. However, under the proposed legislation I would have no way to deal with an unreasonable complaint from an uneducated neighbor.

The rezoning of land for subdivision purposes put small horse farms such as mine at risk. The passing of this kind of law would be an added risk.

Therefore, I do not believe that this law should be passed without further discussion and review.

JA

{2}

I have been reading with growing concern about the proposed changes to the Michigan Right to Farm act. While I understand that the animal industry must be regulated, it is disturbing that the changes seem aimed at removing the ability of small scale farmers to raise their own food. My own business has relied in the past on farmers. Where would we be without those willing to feed us all? And, even more important, where will we be if we lose the ability to feed ourselves?

I have watched rural areas change when small farms have had to sell out to large-scale farming groups, and while good farmland and rural character are lost to the division of property into small parcels. Folks that buy these properties often have little understanding of the way food is grown and produced by farmers large and small. RTF offers farmers a way to protect themselves against individuals and communities that have little appreciation for the process of farming. Why are we talking about taking that protection away from individuals that wish to produce their own food? I would hate to think that such a decision would be based on the needs of corporate farming, or on powerful individuals that for their own reasons think that food production should only [include] plastic wrap and a grocery store.

While it is not possible to make everyone happy all of the time, I hope you will consider how un-American it is to prevent people from supporting themselves in a way that does not endanger the public in any way. Please continue to protect those that wish to support themselves and their families with their own efforts, and decide against the proposed changes to the Act.

Mary M. Alban, DVM

{3}

I would like to voice my concerns over the proposed changes dictating the inability to raise any number of animals where it is deemed residential [Category 4], as well as the proposed classification of the new non-production "Livestock Facilities".

I fail to see how a small number of chickens in a suburban back yard, fenced properly and maintained, could be an issue to any surrounding neighbors. If barking dogs and screaming children are allowed on residential property, I feel it is the right of all human kind to have the ability to both raise animals and farm the land, if properly maintained. No one enforces rules while the neighbor sitting in his driveway with radio blaring and waking up children. You mean to say that a maintained flock of chickens will cause more conflict than loud subwoofers? I disagree.

If you insist on devising rules to enforce these limitations, at least do it responsibly. A small flock of chickens (without any roosters) will make nearly no noise at all, and generate no smell. I can understand placing limitations on larger livestock (i.e. horses and cattle) however some review maybe needed on how the land is currently zoned.

From the dawn of mankind we have been taming, raising and cultivating. There should be no laws in place that would prohibit the expression of our right as a culture to grow our own crops, raise our own food and tend to our animals, if done reasonably and responsibly. In today's society with shootings and crime, I would not think it unfair to deny a child or adult the joy in seeing a crop come to fruition or an animal produce to feed your family. Do not remove their human and genetic right to work their land.

Please think carefully during these discussions as you maybe hurting more small farms and families than you know.

Daniel J. Albin

{4}

I am writing to you to voice my opposition to the proposed changes to small-scale livestock rules in residential areas.

Very few of us, myself included, will ever have the cash to buy a "real" farm. It's my dream that my kids and other children will be able to learn to live farming and engage in producing their own food right at home through 4H.

The proposed set of changes are specifically aimed at stopping that. Please do not go through with it. Farmers are aging, and we need kids to grow up and farm.

Anne Anderson

{5}

This change appears to give favor to big commercial agricultural operators, while harming small farms and individuals who could benefit from greater independence and control of their food supply.

Lynda Anderson

{6}

As the proud owner of four backyard chickens that have enriched my family's life considerably, the proposed changes to Michigan's Generally Acceptable Agricultural Practices are troubling. Urban agriculture has helped us reconnect with the land in a small but beneficial way. It has helped my daughter see where her food comes from & has been a great learning experience not only for her, but for everyone who comes to our home. My neighbors have no complaints & enjoy seeing the chickens & asking about them. Please don't make it harder to do things like this! We should be removing barriers to self-sufficiency, not erecting them.

Tanya Andrews

{7}

I am writing in protest to the proposed changes to Generally Accepted Agricultural and Management Practices for Site Selection and Odor Control for New and Expanding Livestock Production Facilities.

It is unreasonable to place additional limitations onto small-scale agricultural activity, especially those stationed near or within urban limits. Even rural areas now zoned residential are at risk, even if local zoning allows for small-scale agricultural activity. It is a grave mistake to undermine time-honored practices of resilient, distributed food production in relative location to its processing and consumption; the home and local economy.

The foundation of a sustainable and just local food system rests largely on the expression of well-intentioned individuals to exercise their right to produce nutritious animal based foods within communities, so long as proper management is followed. Thus, what is more pertinent an issue regarding food safety and quality of life is the education of the public as to where food comes from and how its local rearing supports local economy and a renewed vitality of the general public through its consumption.

Mark Angelini

{8}

I am writing to you to object to the current proposition to amend the Right to Farm Act to the complete exclusion of farms in residential zones. This affects me and many others on a very personal level.

My 2 acre property and the properties of many other farmers were overtaken by rezoning from Agricultural to Residential due to suburban sprawl. While new neighborhoods grow up and around existing farms, there is no proof that these neighborhoods are in any way endangered by the existence of the farms. My own property was inspected and found to be in compliance with GAAMPs and in no way a risk to the environment or to my neighbors. I am currently able to continue selling my natural, organic eggs from cage free hens to locals who appreciate a healthier and more natural diet. The proposed changes under the Michigan Right to Farm Act would remove protection from my farm solely due to the location, as it is now zoned Residential.

Please consider the long term ramifications of preventing small farms from growing natural, healthy food and relying solely on large, for-profit enterprises to keep everyone fed. Michigan has the best farm protection act in the country. Self-reliance is something to be encouraged, not repressed. The more resources we have as a state, the wealthier we will be, in all ways. Farmers are one of our states greatest resources. Commercial businesses are behind the push to eliminate local farmers to improve their own profits.

When the last small farmer is pushed out by rezoning, and the last tree is cut down for a new neighborhood and the last fish eaten and the last stream poisoned, you will realize then that you can't eat money and you will be forced to subsist on whatever mystery swill out of state for-profit enterprises choose to feed you.

Melissa Arab

{9}

I am writing in opposition to changes that would outlaw livestock in residential areas. There is no reason that a reasonable number of small livestock such as chickens, ducks, turkeys, rabbits, or small goats should be incompatible with a clean and comfortable neighborhood. Given the correct amount of space and care these animals are no more disruptive to residential life than dogs or cats. I hope that you will reconsider the ban and choose a more moderate action.

Alice Bagley

{10}

There are a number of issues related to the proposed changes to the Site Selection GAAMPs:

1. GAAMPs have historically been used to establish guidelines which, if met, earn the farmer protection under the right to farm act. The preface added in 2012, and changes to the Site Selection GAAMPs over the past two years introduce a new kind of requirement which can't be met by any farmer in a residential area. Thus the purpose of this language is not to promote good agricultural management guidelines, but rather to exclude whole classes of farmers from Right to Farm protection. I urge the Ag Commission to turn back from making this kind of a fundamental change to the purpose of the GAAMPs.

2. If the proposed changes to the Site Selection GAAMPs are approved, it will create a conflict between the Right to Farm law and the GAAMPs. The law will prohibit the use of local regulations to supercede RTF, and the Site Selection GAAMPs will require that local zoning supercede RTF, if that zoning is "residential". I expect that most lawyers will be able to explain that conflict to a judge, and that Michigan residents will continue to win Right to Farm cases in Michigan because the law will still protect us, even if this change to the GAAMPs is approved. Still, I urge the Ag Commission to not introduce this conflict between the language of the law and the language of the GAAMPs.

3. One reason given for MDARD pursuing this policy change is that the department is receiving more inquiries from Michigan residents interested in urban and residential agriculture than they can easily handle. This would suggest that it is the express intent of our Department of Agriculture to suppress agricultural efforts in residential areas, where about 80 percent of Michigan residents live. I strongly urge the Ag Commission to not use its authority to thwart agricultural interests among Michigan citizens, but instead to use its authority to promote those interests.

4. A second reason given for MDARD pursuing this policy change is that RTF protection for small farmers could lead RTF back to the

legislature for amendment, and amendments to RTF could hurt other agricultural interests in the state. My own view is that the essential unfairness of the proposed changes to the Site Selection GAAMPs have the same power to bring RTF back to the legislature for clarity on who is protected by Right to Farm. I urge the Ag Commission to not pick winners and losers in an effort stabilize our existing RTF law, both because it is wrong and because it appears unlikely to work.

5. Finally, I would note that there is a real and growing frustration among consumers around our food choices. One way that those concerns can be alleviated without fundamental change is to create greater options for purchasing locally grown foods, and greater options for individuals to grow their own food. Instead, the proposed changes to the Site Selection GAAMPs will have an enormous dampening effect on both of these options, and in my view will lead to greatly increased frustration on the part of Michigan residents. I urge the Ag Commission to promote the kind of small sustainable agriculture that is required to support farmer's markets and the locally grown food movement, by not approving the proposed changes to the Site Selection GAAMPs.

Wendy Lockwood Banka

{11}

As an urban farmer and beekeeper, I strongly protest the proposed changes to the RTFA. MOST people live in cities. If we are to have the right and freedom to produce our own food, we need to do some of that in cities.

Lisa Bashert

{12}

I recently read about proposed changes in agriculture regulations that would define an animal facility as something having as few animals as 1; and then allowing animal facilities in only particular places. I think this is bad for Michigan. Lots of people are now trying out small scale farming and that is a good thing. The proposed changes could certainly be used to bend policy and zoning and more regulations away from small and start up farms. We don't need more CAFOs, we need more farmers who are concerned with local production, and distribution.

People in subdivisions and residential neighborhoods that are "invaded" by farm animals should be able to work out their differences by themselves. Indeed, many site condos and subdivisions have rules that prohibit the keeping of animals except in the most ordinary way, and numbers. I don't think the State needs to address those at all.

Michigan needs small, creative farms, and places where potential farmers can start their projects without having to own a lot of land, or having to give up "day jobs" that are nearby.

Don't make these changes.

Katy Bean-Larson

{13}

I urge you to make no changes to the Michigan right to farm act! My family and many others enjoy the right to raise our own chemical free food and we all know it would be a huge mistake to change that.

I would also hope you consider the recent polls on how 94% of Americans are dissatisfied with our current law makers and that the time has obviously come to do things for the people and not the corporations!

David M Beaudette

{14}

There are plenty of people who depend on their right to farm to sustain their families. I know of a number of them personally. Please reconsider these changes, as they will cause substantial hardship for many in Michigan, including close friends of mine, in already difficult financial times for this state, and the entire country. People have the right to feed themselves, and their families. This should not be stripped from them with such sweeping changes.

Mike Beers

{15}

This is especially distressing to me personally because I strive to find local food sources from ethically responsible farmers. I believe that small scale farming should be allowed to flourish in Michigan as a more sustainable option to provide food for our families. If the proposed GAAMPS changes in site selection are passed, only large-scale farms where questionable farming practices occur in the areas of animal treatment and soil conservation will be favored and the only option for food sources here in Michigan.

Michelle R. Brejnak

{16}

Hello. I am writing in regard to the proposed amendments to the GAAMPs. I am most concerned with the Site Selection revisions. With the current language of the GAAMPs, any farm that is GAAMP compliant and meets the criteria of a "farm" having a "farm product" and being "commercial in nature" are offered Right to Farm protection.

Our story here at Shady Grove Farm U.P. is a perfect example of how the Right to Farm Act can be applied and used as a defense for an Environmentally Verified Farm, producing quality food for the community. Through the MAEAP process, none of the technicians or verifiers had any issue with what we were zoned. That didn't matter to them. What mattered were our farming practices and compliance with the applicable GAAMPs. As a matter of fact, they couldn't believe that anyone would even have a problem with our operation. They thought our farm was very diverse and our practices were exemplary compared to other farms.

When Joe Kelpinski, Erin Satchell and Holly Wendrick got done finalizing the paperwork and had me sign it, in our kitchen, Joe stood up and said, "You now have right to farm protection". At that point, I have no idea if he knew that our township was filing a suit against us or not. But, the point is, he did his job the way it is supposed to be done, he applied the rules as they are supposed to be applied and he told us we have protection via a state law because we were found to meet ALL necessary criteria per the Michigan Department of Ag and Rural Development's own standards. THAT is how the Right to Farm Act is supposed to work.

With the newly proposed language and definitions, in particular the "Livestock Facility" definition, these protections will be wiped out for many Michigan farms due to outdated zoning and local municipalities over reaching their authority. Adding the definition "Livestock Facility" is simply a move to eradicate farms in an urban or rural setting, if not zoned for Agriculture. This would allow local governments to simply change zoning to boost tax revenues and prohibit us, the tax payers, from utilizing our right to farm and our right to choose how we live and what we eat. Changing the number of animals from 5,000 (Livestock Production Facility) to ANY number of animals (Livestock Facility) is ridiculous and completely unnecessary. There is no science based evidence to support these changes, which is what these changes are intended to be based on. If a farm, regardless of zoning, can meet the requirements to be GAAMP compliant per your OWN rules, then why should it matter what zoned district it is in? They are YOUR rules, regulations and standards, after all. In addition, those of us with small operations are much more likely to be environmentally sound.

With the local food movement gaining momentum, with Farmers Markets popping up throughout the state, with tax payers waking up and realizing the importance of healthy food, we NEED small farms. We need MANY small farms to create sustainable, local food systems. There is room in this market for ALL farms. Putting profits aside for a minute, because I know that's what this is really all about (MONEY), let's look at a person's rights. We have the constitutional right to choose what we eat. We have the constitutional right to grow food. And, we have the constitutional Right to Farm. If someone can't be compliant with the applicable GAAMPs, then they are not provided that protection. And, as far as Townships and Cities, they already have a way to introduce zoning that is in direct conflict with the MRTFA. They have to send it to you folks for approval. Yet, no municipalities do that.

Now, aside from the fact that no changes are needed in the language of the Right to Farm Act, or the Site Selection GAAMP, there is this: Your agency can't simply rewrite the law. You only have the authority to carry it out as the legislature intended. If you are going beyond that, you are violating the separation of powers. We must look at the direction that the lobbying from corporate ag is taking our government. You folks work FOR the people. You are required to do what is BEST for the PEOPLE. Stripping tax payers of our constitutional right to be protected by a State Law is not the answer. Providing the protection of the Right to Farm Act for ALL compliant farms IS the answer, which is what the current language of the Right to Farm Act and GAAMPs (Site Selection...) does! These proposed changes will make the country's strongest Right to Farm Act the weakest. The proposed language to the Site Selection GAAMP is a blatant attempt at eliminating small farms in areas that are zoned something other than "agriculture", even if we are compliant with the current GAAMPs. The changes would deem the Right to Farm Act as unconstitutional as it takes away the rights of farmers in non-ag areas.

It is my hope that you as the Commissioners of Agriculture and Rural Development for the State of Michigan will see that these proposed amendments should not be adopted. For the greater good of our people, we must retain the Right to Farm for ALL farms. For the future of farming in Michigan, we must retain the Right to Farm for ALL farms. For the future of food security, we must retain the Right to Farm for ALL farms. Remember, many small farms is a sustainable idea...a few corporate farms is not!

Randy Buchler

{17}

In all fairness, small-scale farming nuisances, residential or otherwise, can be tolerated just as much as lifestyles that convert land use into McMansions and chemical-dependent evergreen lawns.

Please support fair policies.

Mark Bugnaski

{18}

I am respectfully sending my opinion that I am opposed to proposed changes that would allow local units of government to override the Right to Farm Act. I believe the GAAMPS in place are sufficient to control the issues and local governments should not be involved with the process.

I am speaking as both a local elected official of Grand Haven Charter Township and also a concerned resident who believes in self-sustainability for families as well as the belief that if we allow this, we will lose the ability for a person to find truly whole, unprocessed foods that are grass fed and not filled with hormones and the like. There is so much evidence growing that processed foods are the cause behind so many cancers and to not allow people the choice of where and how they get their food would be a huge mistake.

Sue Buitenhuis

{19}

I have attached the current (as of 8:10am) signature & comment list from my petition on Change.org. I implore you & your colleagues to do away with the changes to the site selection GAAMP; specifically the section that deems residential zoned areas unsuitable for the keeping of any (even 1) livestock animals; and the definition of a livestock facility. I assure you that any farm keeping less than 50 (less than 100!) "animal units" is just that—a farm! Not a "livestock facility". Most of the farmers (as opposed to factory running business people) I know are committed to the health & well being of not only themselves, and their animals but to their greater community. They certainly are caring for their animals in much more humane conditions than are outlined as necessary in the "Care of Farm Animals" GAAMP!! (have you even read that document?!? that is "care" of an animal? I think not!).

As to the zoning issue: If you carefully examine, & trace the ownership of much of the "agriculture zoned" areas in the state, you will find that these large parcels of land are owned by big ag, big business. Most of the small family farms are now located in areas deemed "residential" simply due to past political & financial reasons. With the advent of big ag, most traditional family run farms were over time forced to sell off parcel by parcel most of their land simply to continue to live.

Also, as to the people who are raising chickens, bees, rabbits, or even goats in urban or suburban areas, again they are invested in their communities in a way that big ag will NEVER be. These urban farmers often provide education & free food to their community at large. Their ability to supplement their offerings of produce with the addition of eggs, meat, honey & dairy products is a crucial part of providing HEALTHY locally grown food to people who otherwise may not have adequate access.

I wish that you and your colleagues could take the time to visit these people/ farms/ community centers to determine what impact these proposed changes could have on food safety & security in MI. I hope you have done adequate research into the state of food in our state.

Please, again, reconsider the impact your actions will have on the future of our state.

Julie Burkey

{20}

I am writing to voice that I am opposed to changes in policy that restrict the ability to raise livestock in urban/residential areas.

If we are to have a connection with our food system, localized for sustainability, and liberty from reliance on Big Ag, which also requires greater energy/transportation resources; we must have the ability to locally raise and grow our food.

Liz Busch

{21}

I am thoroughly opposed to the creation of Category 4 sites where any livestock enclosure is prohibited. We need to further integrate and imbed agriculture into our townships, not exclude it to the fringes. Residential zoning in townships can sometimes mean parcels of 50, 70 or 100 acres zoned residential. To say a person cannot enjoy RTF protection if he has one animal enclosed is ludicrous. Please do not adopt this proposed change.

Phillip Campbell
Mayor, City of Howell

{22}

I live in Detroit, and one of the bright spots in Detroit is the many small urban farms and gardens which have turned what others considered to be a wasteland of abandonment and vacant land into productive and vital parts of the city. I know of a number of these urban farms where beekeepers are keeping bees, and because of this, urban beekeepers helped to maintain and increase the population of honeybees. As is now common knowledge, honeybees as pollinators are vital to our food supply and the bees are declining in numbers everywhere due to complex reasons. However, most of the beekeepers and bees in the cities are thriving! There are no pesticides and the bees do very well in the "urban prairie" of wildflowers (weeds) on all the vacant land and on the urban farms. Also many of these small urban farms and gardens may have a few chickens or other small farm animals, besides bees.

What you are proposing threatens to put urban farming and urban beekeeping out of business. That is exactly the opposite of what the Right to Farm Act intends. I urge you to reject the proposed changes.

John R. Canzano

{23}

I am greatly stressed over the news that once again a government agency is trying to stop my family from feeding ourselves. Farming is farming regardless of the acreage size or scale. Why would an agency dedicated to farming in the state of Michigan produce a change in our system that would stop us from farming???? I can't seem to come up for an answer to that very question.

Many of us in this state are struggling to make ends meet and the proposed change in the GAAMPs would be catastrophic for us that live in residential areas but yet farm under the GAAMPs system. There are no logical reasons why these changes should be implemented. I strive to maintain a healthy, clean, quiet, and neighbor friendly farm. My neighbors love chickens and buy my eggs and I constantly check with them to make sure that they don't smell or hear anything from our area. I am sure that not all neighbors are like my own and that not all farmers care about what their neighbors think, and in fact could care less about the smells and sounds emitting from their farms. WE DO CARE and we should not be punished because others do not care as we do.

As you know the law reads, changes to the GAAMPs should be based on scientific evidence; no evidence has been provided that supports the current changes to the Site Selection GAAMPs. The law also states that changes to the GAAMPs should be for purposes of improved public health or the environment; no evidence has been provided that small farms in residentially zoned areas are a threat to public health or the environment. Indeed the fact of the matter is that larger CAFOs, better known as "factory farms" actually create more of a danger to the public health and environment and are a far greater source of nuisance to our state than small family farms.

From a legal standpoint the proposed changes create language in the GAAMPs that contradicts the language in the law (that is, the GAAMPs require zoning to regulate Livestock Facilities while the Law prohibits zoning from regulating them). While the Agriculture Committee has the authority to change the language of the GAAMPs, they do NOT have the authority to change the meaning of the law, and that is what this change attempts to do.

The current trend in this country and in our state is to squash small business with unnecessary regulations. Many of these regulations are founded on fear and are written with a lack of attention to the facts at hand . . . this proposed change follows that same trend.

Kimberly Claflin

{24}

The Commission's and the Department's attempts to prohibit urban agriculture has a long history. As long ago as September 2011, the Commission contemplated adopting an "urban agriculture policy statement." That statement included the following language:

> "...it is the policy of the Commission of Agriculture and Rural Development that a *local unit of government may enact a land use zoning ordinance that extends or conflicts with existing GAAMP standards under very strict conditions.*"

Those two conditions were whether the municipality had a population of 50,000 or more, and whether the municipality had established an "overlay zone" pursuant to applicable law. If the two conditions were satisfied, then the Commission and the Department would be sanctioning a "land use zoning ordinance that extends or conflicts with" the RTFA, a clear violation of law because the RTFA expressly provides that it preempts any conflicting local zoning ordinance.

Apparently, that September 2011 "policy statement" was not enough. In December 2011, the Commission modified all of its GAAMPs by including the following language:

> "This GAAMP does not apply in municipalities with a population of 100,000 or more in which a zoning ordinance has been enacted to allow for agriculture provided that the ordinance designates existing agricultural operations present prior to the ordinance's adoption as legal non-conforming uses as identified by the Right to Farm Act for purposes of scale and type of agricultural use."

And now the Commission and the Department wish to totally and completely eliminate urban agriculture with respect to livestock by creating a new "Category 4."

David G. Cox

{25}

I am a concerned business owner who features local ingredients in our breakfasts and desserts for our Bed & Breakfast in Northern Michigan.

These new rules will have a negative effect on many of the farms that I buy food from, my business, my family's ability to find local food, and the environment. I ask you to ensure that new regulations do not put family farms out of business, harm farmers' soil, water, and wildlife conservation efforts, or shut down the growth of local and regional healthy food systems! I raise my own chickens here at the B&B and this would significantly affect my own ability to offer my guests fresh, local and organic eggs each day.

I have a number of friends in the Traverse City area who are farmers, growers and chefs. These "proposed" changes will negatively impact a region that is thriving and is a destination for FOOD. My guests at the B&B come up North to enjoy and support locally grown organic food. I make every effort to purchase local organic produce and support these often family run businesses. If these farmers go out of business, my only alternative would be to use unhealthy processed food. These family run farms also support the local wildlife and are helping to protect and create habitats for bees and other pollinators.

Jamie Creason
Applesauce Inn B&B

{26}

I own 60 acres (middle of no where) and I have 23 chickens (MAEAP VERIFIED). The township still forces me to zone residential (so they can tax me at a high rate) then later comes back and uses the zoning game to extort MORE money from me to have chickens. That issue will be settled in court needless to say.

MDARD needs to realize that every situation is different and should be settled locally. Passing such a rule clearly appears to be a lever pull for Big BUSINESS and a boot in the ass to the everyday citizen. I hope MDARD will re-evaluate its proposed changes and represent THE TAX PAYER in this situation.

John Curtis

{27}

I am writing in to oppose the removal of the protection provided by the Right To Farm Act to farmers and hobbyists living in residential areas. I strongly disagree with the changes and removal of rights to keep livestock and to farm. Please vote no on the proposed changes.

Carole Darby

{28}

I am writing to express my opinion on the Michigan Right to Farm Act. I STRONGLY oppose changes to the Michigan Right To Farm Act. I feel that those in residential areas should retain their rights to raise their own livestock as well as garden.

Tracy Darby

{29}

I would think it would more beneficial to allow the inclusion of small amounts of animals if they comply with generally accepted standards. Small animals such as chickens pose no greater environmental problems than do domestic pets. I believe it is my right to feed myself and to raise my own food without undue interference from regulators.

Donald Day

{30}

Michigan currently has the best Right to Farm Act (RTFA) in the country, and the proposed addition of Category 4 to the Site Selection GAAMP will undermine what the farmers and citizens have fought to keep for decades.

DO NOT add category 4. It WILL come back to haunt you.

There is a reason so many people are against it!

Jeremy Day

{31}

I am writing out of concern about two proposed changes in the 2014 Draft Site Selection & Manure Management Generally Accepted Agricultural Management Practices ("Site Selection GAAMP"). These two changes would undermine the Michigan Right to Farm Act's protection for farmers and others who, I believe, have a right to raise small animals in residential areas.

For more than 25 years I have been involved in local planning – I worked as a professional planner at the regional level for several years, I taught planning at Northern Michigan University for nearly 20 years, and I served on the City of Marquette planning commission for more than 15 years (and more than half of that time as its chair). I have also been actively involved in sustainability issues, especially local food systems, for more than a decade. I am fully aware of the implications the proposed changes to the Site Selection GAAMP would have in the connection between state regulation and local land use control.

I oppose the adoption of language extending the reach of the Site Selection GAAMP to farms with even less than one animal unit. This change would likely abolish any keeping of livestock, even flocks of less than a dozen chickens or one bee hive, in most urban settings because the setbacks would be difficult or impossible to meet there.

This is unnecessary over-regulation that could be avoided by leaving the definition of "livestock production facility" just as it is, or at a minimum, making it applicable at a reasonable number of animal units.

I oppose the changes throughout the Site Selection GAAMP that ban all keeping of animals in residential areas. This change would subject every newly regulated "Livestock Facility" (again, just one animal would qualify) to local zoning restrictions. This change would conflict with the intent of the RTF legislature which intended that local zoning schemes not be able to dictate where or how farming could occur. From a planning perspective, I see a return to chaotic/conflicting zoning requirements emerging at the local level all over the state, directly in opposition to the original intent of RTF, and an immense step backward for food security efforts in Michigan.

Do NOT drop the animal units down to 0 in the definition of a Livestock Production Facility.

Do NOT gut the Right to Farm Act by giving local zoning ordinances the power to control where farming can happen.

The Michigan RTFA is a template for the defense and encouragement of local food production and the restoration of agriculture to its rightful place — integrated into communities.

If Michigan wants true food security — defined as the ability to be as self-sufficient in food production as possible — then we need a legal system that supports local, small-scale food production. Please protect the current integrity of the RTF Act.

Dr. Stephen R. DeGoosh

{32}

I STRONGLY urge you to move away from the proposed "category" classification system. As you are aware, the proposed changes would virtually wipe-out the "backyard" farmer. The (hopefully) unintended consequences of these proposed changes would be that small farmers would be stripped of any protection for their farming operations. The ripple effect of this would affect 4-H and FFA activities, roadside farm stands, and the availability of non-commercially produced fresh eggs and produce, to name a few.

Cheryl DeGroote

{33}

I am writing in support of the CURRENT Michigan Right to Farm act. The roots of our country's history, and our state's history, are within agriculture. It has only been in the last 50 years that this has changed. We have a strong, sustainable farming movement happening all over this state, and we currently are proud of the laws that protect farmers (who are nearly all zoned residential).

I'm concerned with the proposed changes to the GAAMP; they need to be based on science. The current changes appear to not be, and that deeply concerns me as an educator and researcher working at a Michigan University.

Small family farms in residential areas improve public health by access to fresh vegetables, eggs, and so forth – they do not detract. I have several farmers who live on my road, and I am happy to buy produce directly from them, support our local economy, and engage in more healthful eating. I am happy to live in a suburban area that allows for the diversity of farms and healthy living.

I ask, therefore, that you retain the original meaning and intent of the Michigan Right to Farm Act – it is a model for other states, and is allowing Michigan to push ahead with localized, sustainable food systems.

Dr. Dana Lynn Driscoll

{34}

I want to express my support for allowing people in residential neighborhoods to keep chickens, goats or any other animals which are not a nuisance to neighbors. I live in an older neighborhood in downtown Kalamazoo. Our houses are very close together. Several of our neighbors and community gardens keep chickens and bees and some are considering a goat. I work hard to grow a few vegetables for our family and for canning. This ability to save money and to know where your food is grown/cultivated is important to my family and me. My children know where eggs come from as well as their meat. We only buy meat from people we know. They eat very healthy and are always excited to try food they have grown or helped to harvest. Some of the proposed changes to the GAAMP may compromise the rights of those who want to keep 1 or 2 chickens for eggs for their families. Please consider the very small farmer. I want my neighbors to have this right.

Sarah Drumm

{35}

I have invested in acreage in Michigan (Sharon Township) to use for retirement income via small scale beekeeping and farm operations on that particular property.

I have also invested thousands of dollars in beekeeping equipment and have contracts with two small scale farms to provide pollination services. These farms are surrounded by residential areas.

The proposed changes bring operations as small as a single animal under the control of the Site Selection GAAMPs, and then use the new Category 4 definition to exclude those operations from RTF protection in residential areas. It also would allow Sharon Township to decide if ANY farm activities or beekeeping could be allowed on the agricultural property I have-invested in and am paying taxes on. And, the proposed changes jeopardize the operations at the two small scale organic farms that I currently have perpetual pollination contracts with in Ann Arbor and Monroe.

I made the decision years ago to invest my hard earned dollars in these agricultural activities because the fair farming act protected my activities on these properties. Now that several new subdivisions have broken ground in the area of my agricultural property, my retirement income will be in jeopardy, as is my investment in beekeeping equipment and livestock, if the fair farming act is changed as proposed

Judith Durfy

{36}

This is not right, and I'm sure you ALL realize it deep in your hearts. The cost of living is sky high and most food at the local grocery is all CRAP. Forgive my language. I should have access to locally grown, raised eggs, chickens, beef, whatever, grown by caring local farmers who want to provide a much higher quality food for their families and the community.

Wendy Eaton

{37}

While you may believe this is an issue confined to urban areas, please remember that most of our townships are now strictly zoned and those areas historically used as farmland are being rezoned as residential only. Farming has long been considered one of the backbones and prides of Michigan and these changes will only seek to drive more small farms out of the state, especially the younger generation of farmers seeking places where they can work the land while they work professionally.

Multiple urban farm publications, beginning with those produced during the first World War, have emphasized the use of animals to produce healthy soil for growing food. The soil in most Michigan cities is so depleted that it will not support healthy plant life without a serious amount of help. Many of these problems can be solved with properly applied compost consisting of both animal and vegetable waste.

This is also an issue of urban food justice. People in food deserts, like the one I live in, do not have easy access to milk, eggs, and produce. We have the neighbourhood party store and the drug store, and while they both try to keep at least some fresh food on the shelves, they cannot keep up with demand, nor is that their primary mission. People here WANT to produce their own food. I have had so many neighbours ask me for gardening tips, ask if we could give them a little goat milk, or ask if we were ever getting chickens so they could barter for eggs. The urban core is not full of slackers who don't want fresh food, it is full of impoverished people who lack skills and are eager to learn, but are faced with barriers such as getting that soil healthy, or acquiring seeds or seedlings, or, if this passes, the inability to even provide their own proteins, leaving them with the only option being the salt-filled and highly processed deli meats that the party store sells. If people can grow their own food, they will.

We once celebrated city farms. During WWII, the vast majority of US food production was done locally by people in their own yards, and yes, this included farm animals in the city. Cities that want to be attractive and vibrant are bringing this back.

Take this as you will, but I hope my voice joins many in saying that these changes do not reflect what the people in Michigan want- they do not reflect what the people you keep trying to bring back to Michigan want.

And they certainly do not reflect the values of a state that claims to be proud of its farmers and its heritage as one of the food producing superstars of this country.

Anna L. EldenBrady

{38}

I volunteer on two farms within two counties of Michigan. I am well aware that this state is losing its small family owned farms to large corporate farms, housing developments, and/or houses that sit on 10 to 20 acres. Less than 2 percent of our country engages in farming. The new changes are to benefit only those in housing developments and other "residential areas" that do not want to witness a small farm next to them. These proposals turn a blind eye to the people who should be protected. Establishing Category 4 sites, where no agricultural practices can take place, only hurts the farmer. The members of the board who approve such proposals will directly harm the existence of the small family owned farm.

Goose Elliott

{39}

As parents of six children living on a hobby farm in Brandon Township Michigan we urge you to consider the great value that urban and hobby farming offer to the future of Michigan.

Studies support what our family found when we moved from Beverly Hills, Michigan to Brandon and started a 4-H club. Kids involved in the science of agriculture learn responsibility, creativity, technical skills, endurance, marketing, enviro-responsibility, and so many other life skills directly related to their future capacity as adults and the future of Michigan's economy. Our kids will be the adults who will know how to sustain our states need for food and any career that values the above abilities. Agriculture is one of the top industries which contribute to the Michigan economy. Please consider that future farmers aren't made post-college. These green technology adults grow from kids who start with the urban/backyard hobby/4-H farm. In fact, my oldest daughter is now studying Animal Science and Bio-Technology. She will feed you and I through our twilight years! Protect the small farm!

Michelle Ervin

{40}

Homeowners and land owners have the right to raise animals or grow gardens on their property wherever that might be. My neighbor's dog poop smells but I don't want to ban her from having a dog. My neighbor can legally burn leaves that make me absolutely sick so why shouldn't I be able to raise a chicken or two?

Leave small farmers alone. People have the right to grow food.

Katrina Ezbenko

{41}

The environment (and the public) have suffered from legislation restricting individual's rights to procure and create healthy and local food products. GMO's have been introduced into our food source and we do not have the right to be informed so that we can make a decision regarding purchasing. The free market economy does not work when the public is denied the right of information about the products being sold.

The only way to protect ourselves, our children and our community from hazardous decisions made by large corporations is to have the right to produce our own food in our own communities. Altering the Right to Farm Act in any way that diminishes our ability to fight local zoning laws that lean toward development and commercialization of property, denies us one more tool toward keeping our kids and community healthy. Our ancestors understood the necessity and economy of raising a few chickens for eggs and meat, for having bee hives for honey, for raising sheep for wool. Removing the protection that the RTFA gives us would diminish all of us and lead us down the path of dependency on corporate interests that do not have our interests in mind.

Cathie Ferman

{42}

This is a plea for the Department of Agriculture not to pass the proposed changes for GAAMPS.

If the rights of citizens to have back yard farms on a small scale are taken away it directly affects the health of individuals. We would be at the mercy of commercial farming using pesticides, hormones, and antibiotics, not to mention the diseases animals can have and yet are still sold at market.

I really hope this is not the plan, to take away freedoms, put our health in jeopardy and expose us to unhealthy meats and dairy, and more GMO foods.

Susan Fisk

{43}

I ask that you ask yourself, if we are balancing rights, then shouldn't the Right to Grow Food and maintain control of your health trump the right of a neighbor to stick their nose in your business?

Belinda Fitzpatrick

{44}

I am writing to express my displeasure with the heavy-handed over reach of the proposed site selection GAAMP revision. It is ahistorical and deferential to municipal NIMBYism that refuses to work with and respect people's need to use their properties in a more self-sustaining manner, even in the city.

Please do not issue a blanket proclamation that determines the GAAMP will not apply to residentially-zoned areas.

Karen Francis-McWhite

{45}

I am writing in opposition to proposed changes in the GAAMPs that will outlaw farm animals in residential neighborhoods.

As an urban farmer I take pride in the great services that I can provide to my family and friends in the form of healthy local food. I can take pride that the food that I produce is produced in a sustainable, healthful, and respectful manner. It is a great experience for our kids to understand how to raise animals and to know where their food is coming from, as well as all the kids in the neighborhood that enjoy spending time in our yard.

As a chicken owner I can verify that my small flock is quiet, clean and productive. We live in harmony with our neighbors and share our knowledge freely with all.

The right to produce healthful and sustainable food should be a part of all communities. Legislation should be designed to expand, not limit urban agriculture.

The local food movement is a huge part of our state's food security which will only make Michigan stronger and a more desireable place to live.

Hether Frayer

{46}

I must voice my concern and opposition to the proposed Site Selection GAAMPS as currently outlined. There are numerous reasons for this, culminating in an imminent threat to landowner rights.

There exists NO scientific data to support any of these changes. To be clear, more data exists to ENCOURAGE small scale food production, rather than inhibit it. More locally raised foodstuffs help to stabilize the economy (income for locals, the ability to raise food for those who might night otherwise be able to purchase as many quality foodstuffs), lessen pollution (less trucking of goods over already burdened roads and rails), and, indirectly, increase the health of the population by encouraging them to be more active (one must be at least minimally active to raise even chickens and some garden plants).

The document creates contradictions that fly in the face of landowner rights and common sense. During WW2, ALL citizens, including city dwellers, were encouraged to raise as much of their own food as possible, thereby freeing up resources for the troops, and lessening strain on the US infrastructure. Citizens were encouraged to grow what they could, and trade or buy from locals who grew what they couldn't. This not only helped to feed America in a troubled time, it also encouraged a sense of community and got neighbors to actually get to know one another, which helped to knit a more stable societal fabric. Michigan should be leading the way BACK to this atmosphere, not AWAY from it.

Sam Frazier

{47}

Hello. I am concerned for my right to farm act protection. I am a 6th generation farmer here. We have been here since the 1850's and have had livestock all the while. I purchased 5 acres from my grandfather so I could live and work on our family farm. Not by our choice, but the township zoned it residential property when we broke it off of a 40 that was agricultural. I built a barn and keep horses and calves on my 5 acres. If my family is not protected by the right to farm act with our livestock, then who is it protecting? I love our property and like to live here, but we live near other homes and we need this protection.

Christopher Gallup

{48}

As the country becomes more urbanized, with an ever increasing proportion of the population living in cities, it is important that society remains connected to its food supply and the natural world. Small urban farmers continue the tradition in this country of the self-reliant, can do spirit. Such activities provide an opportunity to teach our children that our food comes from the earth, not a grocery store freezer. Small farmers maintain a connection to our society's agricultural past, but more importantly they are establishing an essential path toward a sustainable future.

Brent Geurnik

{49}

It is imperative that Michigan families have the right to produce their own food on their own property. The changes being proposed to this are detrimental to many Michigan families. The intended benefit is less of a benefit than the damage it would cause so many people in this already economically depressed state. Unlike most rhetorical labels the government designates, Farm Freedom is what this is all about... the freedom to farm! The obligation of governmental agencies is to protect freedom and to encourage production from citizens contributing to their communities, counties, and states, NOT to hamper peoples' efforts to lawfully provide for their family. The proposed changes here are oppressive, unjust, and have no place on the table. There are laws that enslave people, and laws that set them free. Make the right choice.

That is, after all, what we have a government for . . . to protect our rights, not diminish them.

Aaron Gluchowski

{50}

I'm reaching out today to voice my concern over the new proposal for the Site Selection GAAMPS. I do not believe that we should restrict an individual's right to having a few chickens or goats, or other small number of livestock, to help feed and support their families. Besides the fact that animals have been raised in urban settings for ages – people need access to food – there is a desire for folks to have connection with their food, and a desire to have access to healthy, well-raised food – not the food that comes out of factory farm operations.

Please consider both urban livestock, and also small farms, and be considerate of how we can be supportive of raising food in a way that does not require large doses of antibiotics, or raising animals in conditions that would disgust most people, and is the real contributor of pollution in our livestock production. Please go after the operations that are the big time polluters, instead of focusing energies on over-regulating a person's food sovereignty.

Kirk Green

{51}

We raise chickens and grow vegetables. Our farming practices are in absolute compliance with all GAAMPs as well as local noise, odor, and aesthetic ordinances. Our neighbors buy eggs from us, as do people we attend church with. My four year old son loves his chickens and has a better understanding of where his food comes from because of our small farm. He is learning the value of hard work, money, and safe, humane farming. We have invested a great deal of money building the coop, buying supplies, ensuring they are warm through the winter, and now, if these proposed changes are voted for, I will be out the initial investment, the opportunity to teach my son about farming, and that portion of our families income.

Adam Greenwald

{52}

Besides unnecessarily endangering the growth of small-scale ag in areas such as ours here in the U.P., the ambiguous language potentially creates a nightmare scenario of lawsuits and conflict, which neither small rural townships such as ours and many others in the UP nor small-scale farmers can afford to litigate. As one who has been involved with the creation and enforcement of township zoning for many years, I have seen what poorly-worded laws can do. As a Conservation District employee who is trying to expand local agricultural activities, I also am concerned about limiting the expansion of our regionally-sourced food and of our agricultural opportunities here in the UP.

Teri Grout

{53}

By excluding residential property owners from RTF protection, MDARD is going to put many farmers markets out of business. Many government officials including Senator Debbie Stabenow, and Governor Rick Snyder agree that farmers markets are good for Michigan's economy, tourism, and encouraging residence in the state. Michigan's Right To Farm Act currently protects ALL farmers superseding local ordinances against farming.

Many people think of residential zoning to be inner city urban property owners. Realistically there are residentially zoned properties of 500+ acres. Some of these residentially zoned properties are farmed. With agriculturally zoned property decreasing every year to make room for residential property, farm land is getting rezoned to residential all the time. If this site selection GAAMPS is changed, this will exclude protection for many rural farmers. Please consider keeping the current site selection GAAMPS. RTFA protection is sometimes the only protection farmers have against townships trying to keep us from farming through rezoning.

Deanna Gualtieri

{54}

On behalf of Oakland County Poultry Club we would like to express our concerns with possible changes to Michigan's GAAMP. The changes that are being considered will severely restrict the rights of Michigan farmers, particularly small scale farmers. As a supporter of Michigan 4H and farmers in general, we would like to bring to your attention that often times it is the simple "backyard" experience and connection with animals that creates the wonderful lifelong understanding and responsibility of animal ownership. Please do not make any changes and jeopardize the wonderful experience that so many 4H children receive from being able to raise a few chickens, goats or rabbits in their own backyard.

Susan H

{55}

I am writing on behalf of Michigan farmers who are acutely concerned about two proposed changes in the 2014 Draft Site Selection & Manure Management Generally Accepted Agricultural Management Practices ("Site Selection GAAMP"). These two changes would undermine the Michigan Right to Farm Act's protection for farmers.

As a small farmer myself and an attorney who represents small farmers, including those who can continue to farm thanks only to the Right To Farm Act, I assure you that small farms are critical to the financial and physical vitality of communities across Michigan. Small farmers form a vibrant portion of the overall community giving hands-on farming classes, providing goods to consumers and fueling lively farmers' markets. Small farms are bastions of teaching the next generation how to farm. The Right to Farm Act is lauded nationally as an act to emulate for the encouragement and success of farming. Farmers need you to protect its integrity.

First, we oppose the adoption of language extending the reach of the Site Selection GAAMP to farms with even less than one animal unit:

> Livestock Facility – Any facility where farm animals as defined in the Right to Farm Act are confined regardless of the number of animals. Sites such as loafing areas, confinement areas, or feedlots which have any number of livestock that preclude a predominance of desirable forage species are considered a part of a livestock facility.

2014 Draft Site Selection GAAMP, definitions. The addition of this definition would make the Site Selection GAAMP requirements applicable to the smallest of farms. Even a home with one chicken would be required to meet the setbacks of this GAAMP. This change would likely abolish any keeping of livestock, even flocks of less than a dozen chickens or one bee hive, in most urban settings because the setbacks would be difficult or impossible to meet there. We believe that this is unnecessary over-regulation that could be avoided by leaving the definition of "livestock production facility" just as it is, or at a minimum, making it applicable at a reasonable number of animal units.

Second, we oppose the changes throughout the Site Selection GAAMP that ban all keeping of animals in residential areas:

> Category 4 Sites: Sites not acceptable for New and Expanding Livestock Facilities and Livestock Production Facilities. Category 4 Sites are sites that are exclusively zoned for residential use and are not acceptable locations for livestock facilities regardless of number. Confining livestock in these locations does not conform to the Siting GAAMP.

2014 Draft Site Section GAAMP, p. 12. This change would subject every newly regulated "Livestock Facility" (again, just one animal would qualify) to local zoning restrictions. This change would preclude kids across the state from having even one animal for the county fair. Surely this is not your intent, but it would just as surely be a result.

This change gives the power to control where farming can and cannot occur to each city, township or village. This change is in direct conflict with the plain language of the Right to Farm Act:

> Beginning June 1, 2000, except as otherwise provided in this section, it is the express legislative intent that this act preempt any local ordinance, regulation, or resolution that purports to extend or revise in any manner the provisions of this act or generally accepted agricultural and management practices developed under this act. Except as otherwise provided in this section, a local unit of government shall not enact, maintain or enforce an ordinance, regulation or resolution that conflicts in any manner with this act or generally accepted agricultural and management practices developed under this act.

MCL 286.474(6)(emphasis provided). The legislative intent of this amendment to the Right to Farm Act is obvious: the legislature intended that local zoning schemes not be able to dictate where or how farming could occur.

To the extent that the Site Selection and Odor Control of New and Expanding Livestock Facilities GAAMPs changes purport to require compliance with local zoning, that portion of the GAAMP would be in direct conflict with the RTFA's specific and deliberate language to the contrary, MCL 286.474(6), and would be invalid.

Michelle Halley

{56}

I hereby profess my disapproval of modifying Michigan's GAAMPs for the purpose of limiting urban and suburban farms from keeping small numbers of farm animals on their property. While I fully support animal rights and strongly disapprove of any human who would keep animals in areas that are too small or unsafe for the species, I do not believe that further regulation limiting the ability of Michigan citizens to take an active role in their food production, entrepreneurship and our connection to nature, will benefit us in any way.

As for zoning regulations, I strongly believe that any area designated as Residential property inherently allows for the owners/renters of such property to do whatever they deem necessary to ensure the health and happiness of themselves and their families, and raising appropriate numbers and species of farm animals is a wonderful way of doing so.

Katie Hamelin

{57}

Around the country and around the world, the need for food sustainability has inspired changes in local ordinances and enforcement to allow more small-scale urban agriculture, including keeping small numbers of domestic farm animals – especially small ones such as chickens.

It's easy to place regulations that prevent these small food-producing operations from becoming a nuisance — outlawing roosters or regulating food storage, for example — without banning them altogether.

Our daughter Louise Hanavan fought for and eventually won the right for people in Halifax, Nova Scotia, to keep chickens within the city. Her three hens were less noisy and produced less waste than the dogs that she and her husband keep perfectly legally; the chickens benefitted their garden by eating bugs and fertilizing the ground directly; their additional feed was kept in a secure bin, unlike many of the bird feeders that create some attraction to mice and rats; and each hen laid a healthy and delicious egg each day.

To me, these small farms serve only to improve the environment and public health, and the Department of Agriculture should be encouraging them and educating people about their benefits.

Patricia Relf Hanavan

{58}

The proposals to change the RTFA could negatively impact my local organic farmer and his right to provide local real food to folks like my neighbors and me. I want to have farmers close who can provide real food.

Lauren Klaus Habsburg

{59}

Right to Farm should be left intact. There are small businesses in Michigan that we support in their efforts to provide local food. Your committee's recommendation will put them out of business.

Michelle Hazard

{60}

I am writing in regard to The Michigan Right to Farm Act GAAMP Proposed Changes that would strip small farmers in Michigan of certain protections against nuisance complaints from residential neighbors. I strongly oppose the removal of these protections. Such protections keep local communities from favoring larger commercial developmental interests over small farmers. At a time when communities need to look to a variety of places to raise revenue, I fear that such interests could cause local municipalities to push small farms out of the area in order to develop land for residential and commercial purposes.

I am concerned about the impact this might have on even smaller urban farmers. In the last couple of years, parts of Lansing (particularly on the east and south sides) have been transformed by urban farmers. Abandoned lots have been repurposed so that small amounts of crops such as corn, potatoes, lettuce, herbs (and a variety of other plants) can be grown. This not only leads to more available, healthy food in the city, but also gives residents an opportunity to interact with their neighbors and better their neighborhoods. I would hate to see protections taken away that would make this sort of thing more difficult for city residents. It is my hope that the commission rejects these proposed changes, and keeps the protections for small farms in place.

Kristen Heine

{61}

My biggest issue with the proposed change is the language: "sites that are exclusively zoned for residential use . . . are not acceptable locations for livestock facilities regardless of [the] number [of livestock]. Confining livestock in these locations does not conform to the siting GAAMP."

This would mean even a home in a residentially zoned area with ONE COW for the purpose of producing a healthier milk option for their family would be shut down! As someone with a digestive disease (ulcerative colitis) I am very upset about this. I often purchase milk and dairy goods from small residential farmers because I know that the cow was not given chemical laden corn feed, hormones, antibiotics, etc. When I consume dairy products that are free from these chemicals, my digestive system is healthier. AND when I buy them locally I not only know where my food came from but I am helping our local economy.

I can understand not wanting a CAFO (confined animal feeding operation) with many livestock in a residential area, but saying a single cow or a few chickens is a threat to public health or the environment is both false and irresponsible. I would be happy to provide you with actual research showing why this change your propose will damage our economies, negatively impact the health of our citizens as well as lower property values in large urban areas. Please-don't make these changes.

Rachael Hilliker

{62}

I am strongly opposed to the proposed changes to the Generally Accepted Agricultural Practices with the addition of Category 4. These changes will limit the ability of citizens of the State of Michigan to exercise rights to use of their own property. Further, it will prevent residents from having the ability to provide for themselves. Through property rights, people should be able to use their property to provide food for their own family or generate income as they see fit.

Our government should not be in the position of forcing families to purchase food at a store when they can produce it on their own.

Chris Hinkley

{63}

I am a small farmer with a backyard flock of chickens. The changes that are being proposed, which would eliminate any protection for those of us keeping chickens in residential areas greatly concerns me.

The Michigan Department of Agriculture seems to think that removing these protections will benefit the environment, and reduce nuisance issues in neighborhoods. I would like to address these claims. First of all, I think it is a little hypocritical to claim to be helping the environment by eliminating the small flocks that help provide food with much less environmental impact than the large poultry farms do. There is a reason the Right to Farm Act exists, and part of that reason is that large industrial farms smell. Manure lagoons, and hazardous levels of ammonia in chicken confinement houses represent practices in industrial agriculture that are damaging to the environment. Small flocks of chickens like mine, do not stink up the neighborhood. Studies have been done that show that 11 chickens produce about as much manure as one dog. My small flock creates as much manure as my neighbors two dogs, and I take care of it more effectively because I treasure it as a resource for my garden. I trap that chicken waste with wood shavings that cut the smell and bind with the manure making for nice smelling coop that reminds one of a pile of wood, rather than a gaseous swamp or a chemical factory.

I see the small backyard flocks of our state as the lemonade stands of the farming world, how can we expect young people to decide to pursue farming as a career. Urban gardening and farming has produced wonderful results in rough areas of Detroit where I have seen firsthand neighborhoods transformed by people putting down roots with community gardens, and raising chickens on their small plots.

I think more education about keeping chickens should be offered, rather than a restriction of a basic freedom to keep animals for companionship and sustenance.

David Holcomb

{64}

I'm writing to ask you to vote no on any changes to the right to farm act. The proposal states that "sites that are exclusively zoned for residential use . . . are not acceptable locations for livestock facilities regardless of [the] number [of livestock]. Confining livestock in these locations does not conform to the siting GAAMP." In other words, those with livestock on land exclusively zoned for residential use will no longer be protected by RTFA. The changes would affect our backyard flock of chickens and our friends and neighbors who have backyard chicken flocks.

The right to have these small backyard flocks should not be taken away. We've enjoyed many benefits from our small flock. These include a measure of self sufficiency, the joy of caring for the animals, increased communication with our neighbors as they also enjoy the benefits of the eggs. I would hate to see this change. Please do not take away our right to have farm animals in an area zoned for neighborhoods.

Beth Hubbel

{65}

I live in Williamston. If you've never been there, it's quite rural. Until just a few weeks ago we had one traffic light. So we're upscale now, we have two traffic lights.

The city of Williamston itself has until about a year ago passed zoning regulations that allow any farm animal, even cows, in the city. I am in the unfortunate circumstance that I live three houses outside the city in a high density residential area. In this high density residential area of 70 acres there are six houses, and a 40-acre crop farm across the street from us. We have a farm with 20 hens, eight ducks, and two miniature goats. We got the written support of all our neighbors. We have people that walk by our house, we have a sidewalk that runs along the side of our house, and people walk their dogs, and they come and talk to us about our animals and they want to pet the goats.

So we're trying to do a lot of good for our community, and still because of the way that they're trying to change the GAAMPs, our township believes that they are in the right and they have told us that we cannot have our farm and we are under pending litigation for that currently. Our court case should culminate next month.

The GAAMPs are already stacked against pasture-based and organic farming, in other words, small farming. And these changes are targeting small farms and they should not be passed.

Jessica Hudson

{66}

My wife and I own a farm called Hunter Family Farms, which also includes an apiary. My wife and I purchased that farm with the goal of teaching our young children how to grow food and the fiscal responsibility of operating their own business. They raise a small flock of chickens to sell the eggs, and it's been an amazing success to watch them keep track of their expenses and inventory, and care for the animals and teach their friends. My sons are age six and nine. I can't begin to explain the level of responsibility they have gained from this experience. Rather than frequently playing video games, they are outside maintaining life and giving back to others.

Following neighbor complaints, we were directed to the Right to Farm Act. We underwent inspections and made changes to ensure that we were not harming the land and water, and that we were following odor management practices with our entire small acreage farm. This is beneficial to both the small farmer and to the neighbors as a way to ensure harmony. It allows people to grow food to sell to others. It contributes to the local economy as grain and supplies are purchased, and it gives farmers directions to help ensure they're being good stewards of the environment and good neighbors. It helps the state by keeping the ground water safe and the air cleaner, and by keeping future farmers in the know through the ability to grow and to give back products that people want locally. We are one of many success stories of this program, and of the benefits of having these GAAMPs in place.

Please do not implement the proposed changes that bring small farms into the site selection GAAMPs, and then create a new Category 4 that would take people in residential areas not zoned for agriculture use out of the equation. This is Michigan, Pure Michigan, and a change like this will hurt organizations like 4-H and community programs like farmers markets. There are many many residentially zoned properties with enough acreage to support small farms.

David Hunter

{67}

I am greatly involved in 4-H. Last year I was a treasurer, and I am currently the secretary. I raise sheep to show in the fairs. With the money from selling the sheep I was able to purchase a rescue horse. I have fallen in love with the farm life. It is a great comfort and peace to me in the midst of a sometimes crazy world. I can't imagine not having my animals, especially my horses. The animals, especially the horses, bring out an important side of me that very few people see. Please do not make these changes that leave us unprotected.

AnnaLisa Johnson

{68}

It does not seem right for an individual who only has one farm animal to have to comply with the same regulations as those who have 500. Financially that can be impossible for the small hobby farmer or parent who simply wants to give their children a hands on learning experience to better understand what is involved in raising part of their own food. I do not see how this would be supportive of the future development of the agriculture arena in Michigan.

Kathy Johnson

{69}

I am writing to oppose the planned changes in the GAAMPS Site Selection and the resulting outlawing of livestock in residential areas.

Small scale food production can be logical, economical, environmentally friendly, and can feed a lot of people in dire situations. As the GAAMPS are currently written, they assure that the people operate in a way that does not interfere with neighbors and operations do not threaten health or the environment.

There is no logical reason to change the current wording. It seems as though big Ag has too much money and is greedy for more. It is really not okay to bully around the small farmers who are just trying to feed their families and make a living for themselves.

Wendy Johnson

{70}

Hello Michigan! We just moved here Thanksgiving Day. Yes, we moved in during a snow storm in Interlochen, MI. Why do we think Michigan would be a good place to live? Because we plan on farming, improving the land using best permaculture practices, changing from consumers to producers, not being extractive people (people who only use of the resources of the planet) but people who give back to the natural world more than we take. Yes, that is possible.

There are many like us who are already trying to do that. But what does Michigan want to do now? Stop us from that. Many people cannot afford to live on land that is not zoned residential. But they want animals. Why is MDARD trying to mess with that? What exactly is wrong about having animals on a residential lot? Oh, I know. Agribusiness does not want this trend to continue, that of ordinary people taking back their lives to escape the tyranny of factory farmed and produced food.

Janet Joscelyne

{71}

I do not support bringing operations as small as a single animal under the control of the Site Selection GAAMPs. While I understand the need for restrictions in residential neighborhoods with small lots, I believe that any lot over 2 acres has the right to be self sufficient, including the right to raise small animals.

Our citizens should have the right to move more toward localization and away from Globalization. This should include small scale farming, small animals, and renewable energy sources. Our government should be supportive of this strategy and do all it can to protect existing rights.

Jim Kacanowski

{72}

Keepa you hands off the Michigan R.T.F.A. :)

I just found out about proposed changes to the GAMPs governing the "Right to Farm" here in Michigan. I'd like further clarification about how this works exactly. I'm specifically wondering if MDARD was at one point asked to create the GAAMPs and then the state legislature voted to pass the RTFA based on the GAAMPs at the time of creation or whether the legislature agreed to pass the RTFA with the understanding that governing GAAMPs can be modified at any point in the future without further debate?

As a backyard farmer I can attest that we are meeting current GAAMPs standards and our experience (and those of our neighbors) has been of IMPROVING soil quality, IMPROVED HEALTH, IMPROVED QUALITY OF LIFE, and INCREASED WEALTH, apparently much to the chagrin of factory farmers. Speaking of that, perhaps you can apprise me of the outcome of said meeting on Jan 22nd and tell who and what's behind the proposed changes. Was it agribusiness concerns or municipal leadership or their lobbyists (or all of the above)?

Fred Kaluza

{73}

We have two small children ages 5 and 7. We are so proud to be able to provide them with the experience of knowing, raising, and handling small animals. We share the chicks with their classrooms and the teachers love it. Our son showed a chicken at the county fair last year. These are memories that are priceless! These experiences should not be limited to children who grow up on large farms. This is the heritage of our past and we are trying to keep it alive for this and future generations.

Tom and Cathy Keller

{74}

I am writing as a Michigan resident who has no stake in farming other than to provide my family with good food and good health.

I live in a small city at a great distance to most farms. My access to fresh, local food comes from my weekly farmers market as well as other area farmers markets.

Food safety is important to me. Local business is important to me. Being able to purchase wholesome food grown using methods I prefer should be a possibility for ALL Michigan residents. Being able to speak to the farmer is a value that cannot be put into numbers.

There is a great movement of people who are taking their food safety into their own hands and growing for themselves. This should be admired and encouraged.

Please reconsider your recommendations that would put small farms out of business and/or practice.

To this "ordinary citizen" it would appear that you are paving way to give a great advantage to large corporation farms.

Do not treat small farms like large corporate farms. Small farms are not a nuisance to society like large corporation farms are. Small farms were once a part of the great foundation of this country. It would be shameful to put more impediments in the small farmer's way.

Karen Kmieciak

{75}

You cannot take away individuals right to raise livestock in their residential yards. Not everyone has access to land agriculturally zoned or to quality food for that matter. What you're considering is wrong. With so many people out of work right now in Michigan, any effort at self sustainabilty should be encouraged, not legislated against. Keep your hands off of urban agriculture. Direct your efforts towards something worthwhile to the benefit of MI. The only restrictions on livestock that I support would be animal per sq ft, and sanitation requirements. Anything else is just plain unlawful.

Padraic J Ingle

{76}

The more people that grow organic, the more people that are eating it and producing it and it's available to people, the cheaper that's going to become. And I want that food revolution to continue. I have a right to eat what I choose. If you, or you, or anybody else out there chooses to eat GMOs, good for you, that's your choice, knock yourself out. I don't choose to do that. It sounds like most people here don't as well, and I think we have a right to do that.

Julie Liberti

{77}

I am deeply concerned about the proposed changes to Michigan's Generally Acceptable Agricultural Practices (GAAMPs) currently under review. By denying those that live in more dense areas the opportunity to raise animals and use animal bi-products for their families personal use, the Michigan Agricultural Commission will be greatly harming Michigan families. In a world where it is getting more and more difficult to purchase (or afford for that matter) foods that can be trusted as safe, it is imperative the government not meddle in an individual's right to provide for their family.

I would contend that having a few chickens in one's back yard is no more of an inconvenience to neighbors than someone having a few dogs and municipalities like Ferndale and Ann Arbor have shown that it can be done well. I have no problem with regulation, but I do have a problem with an uncreative and unresponsive governments making "one size fits all" policy for the sake of convenience. I realize that it is difficult to make decisions that are inclusive, but that doesn't mean that it shouldn't be done.

Meredith Long

{78}

Many here in southeast Michigan have relied on The Michigan Right to Farm Act to be able to have farm animals which provide their families with food that they know is healthy and free from chemicals that a family member or members may not have a tolerance for. Many people like myself have chosen to have small farm animals because of health problems that have been caused by diets containing chemicals that are in foods purchased from big producers.

Martin Loose

{79}

The proposed changes to the Site Selection GAAMPS directly impact us as our township has arbitrarily, without scientific justification, decided that

1. All regions in Lincoln Township are zoned residential, business or industrial, and

2. No farm animal can be kept on a plot less than 5 acres.

If the Site Selection GAAMPS are changed, then the situation in this rural township will be that you cannot have any number of animals, chickens or otherwise, on a plot of land under 5-acres.

Jenny Lowe

{80}

Please do not change the MDARD terminology of "livestock facility" to apply to anything less than 50 animals.

Please protect the rights of urban homes to keep backyard chickens & a reasonable amount of farm animals to be self sustainable.

Please do not strip the small farms of their right to be protected by state law.

Bethany Lundquist

{81}

This law has been effective, and does not need to be changed.

The landowner has rights superior to his neighbors' rights.

PM

{82}

We the people and citizens of Michigan should not be prevented from growing our own food or raising small animals (such as chickens, turkeys, goats, sheep, rabbits, etc.) to feed us and our families. There was a time when self sufficiency was promoted by our government. This change in Agricultural law will make people more dependent on government and move citizens further away from taking care of themselves and their land.

Jennifer Mannino

{83}

Please know that I am in favor of backyard hens in residential neighborhoods. The changes to the law will prevent my family, and others, from having access to a healthier option while preventing my children from an educational opportunity like no other. While my neighborhood currently prohibits backyard hens, many communities throughout the state allow them and my community is going through the steps to allow a few hens. While I understand that some feel it is unsanitary or that there will be noise and odor issues, most families take exceptionally good care of their animals. In cases where this is not the issue there are usually mandates in the laws put forth in those communities. Please reconsider these changes so that families can have options.

Tammy Mayrend

{84}

I believe it is very important at this time in our State's history to protect everyone's right to grow their own food. We have many issues with food safety, healthy food choices and food access. Please do not vote to change our right to farm.

Jeff McCabe

{85}

Leave GAAMP alone. These changes undermine the very protection put in place for our RIGHT TO FARM ACT.

How many times do the people need to speak for you to hear us?

Heather McDougall

{86}

I am a supporter of the Michigan right to farm act and I urge you to keep it intact.

Mike McGowan

{87}

I am writing in regards to the proposed change to the Michigan Right to Farm Act.

America was built on the agricultural industry, and Americans have sustained themselves in good times and hard times since the Great War of 1918.

We, as citizens are not threat to large farms. If we choose to go out and collect eggs from our own birds it doesn't mean we don't support our local grocery, our local farmers. It means we choose to teach our kids about where their food comes from. The chickens eat bad bugs, fertilize our land and make no noise. Please do not take away a very simple right that truly doesn't cause any harm.

Do not let them remove the right to farm act!

Amy McIntire

{88}

Please do not throw a large, unformed "solution" at a few issues with agricultural/residential problems... we need to encourage backyard chickens and well-run small scale farms in residential areas if we are going to feed ourselves well.

Laura Meisler

{89}

I am a Redford Twp resident, Registered Nurse and a solid advocate for small-scale urban agriculture. Being a home care nurse in Detroit for 6 years prompted me to address the root cause of so many of the diseases we are "fighting" with medications and health care dollars. One of the HUGE root factors of illness of all types is lack of nutrition. There is a severe nutritional desert in many areas in Wayne county (Detroit).

Please please please help encourage the area towards a state of health by letting citizens with no solid way to provide for themselves, raise food for their families in their backyards. This help may look like a garden, or a dairy goat or a beehive. I'm not advocating for large-scale urban agricultural for people to become wealthy from or create a disgusting neighborhood mess. I'm advocating for spreading the concept that even when life has left you without anything, you can always plant a garden, raise a few animals and provide for your family.

Many neighbors and people in this area depend on food stamps, cash assistance and unemployment that will be ending soon. These neighbors and friends have kids they are responsible to provide for. Please give them access to more then pop, chips and liquor. Please enable our area to grow what it can (hens or goats or produce), where it can, in socially responsible ways.

We need access to healthy food. Many neighbors do not have working cars. Yes this is a sad state, but even in this state there is hope...an organic, well managed garden. A few hens to lay eggs year round. This can be a huge asset- empowering citizens with the right to make something from nature's resources.

I am not asking for a government hand out, I am asking for the opportunity for my neighbors and friends to provide for themselves and their families and set a good example of working to provide food for their children (as opposed to creating a culture of people who expect to live off "the system"). There may not be jobs, there may not be much money, but we can always have a garden and a few small animals to provide some solid nutrition.

If it is not clean and sustainable, it shouldn't exist. The same goes for governing policies. Please encourage policies that help us to be nutritionally sustainable.

Jennifer Mergos

{90}

I would like to comment on the proposed change to the Site Selection GAAMP with regards to changing the definition to include sites where animals "are confined regardless of the number of animals." This change in definition from the current use of "animal units" to any amount of animals becomes damaging to property owners with the proposed creation of "Category 4" by saying that these areas are no acceptable to livestock. This change would allow government to take away the ability of property owners to produce their own food.

I do not believe these proposed changes reflect the original intention of Michigan's Right to Farm Act. Michigan is known as an agricultural state. If these changes are passed they would result in limitations to the creation of new farm business and would greatly restrict the ability of people to grow their own food.

Jason Mittlestat

{91}

In reference to GAAMP Site Selection and Odor Control for New or Expanding Livestock Facilities, I oppose the inclusion of Category 4 sites. Factors such as lot size and number of livestock are taken into account by city zoning ordinances. That level of detail in the regulations should be addressed at the local level, not at the state level. There are residential areas where small numbers of livestock can and are being properly kept for the production of healthy food for local families. Decisions about the appropriateness of such land use should be made at the local governmental level.

MerriKay Oleen-Burkey

{92}

I am writing to voice my objection to the language in the proposed 2014 Site Selection GAAMP pertaining to Category 4 sites. Categories 1, 2, and 3 are related both to density of nonfarm residences near the farm as well as number of animal units. The same should be true of Category 4, if defined. Without Category 4, the restrictions of Category 3 are a sufficient restriction as revised.

If altered, this definition would make our rural (no neighbors within 3/4 mile as the crow flies, approximately 200 residents in the entire 36 square mile township and 2/3 of the land is owned by the state) RESIDENTIAL 40 acres ineligible as a suitable place to keep a chicken, turkey, horse, steer. There is NO sound scientific basis in tying zoning to siting. A "residential" zoning does not mean that an area is suitable for constructing a residence, nor that it is inappropriate for other uses. It is merely an indication of potential land use. There are many more factors involved in siting than a tag on an assessor's map.

More time should be spent in considering what the objections are to the keeping of livestock in primarily residential areas. The keeping of animals, whether cat, dog, rabbit, horse, fowl, goat, sheep, cow or any other, should take into account several things: The ability of the site to support the health and welfare of the animal with protection from the elements, proper housing for the type of animal, provision of wholesome feed and water, protection from predators, prevention of vermin, and proper disposal of dead animals and animal waste without offense to immediate neighbors. The Animal Care and Manure Management GAAMPs address these concerns. Conformance with existing and well established scientific principles of livestock management is desirable. In fact, most small farmers provide far more than the published minimum guidelines supported by the state as good management guidelines, especially where floor space, lighting, and ventilation are concerned.

No one is promoting a 1000 bird broiler facility in a subdivision backyard. But the ability to keep half a dozen or a dozen hens for the purpose of selling eggs or breeding rare varieties, or raising a clutch of turkeys for market, or keeping a backyard goat for milk and cheese, should be within the ability of anyone who can properly provide the necessary living conditions and can properly care for the animals and maintain the facility so that it is not objectively harmful to those around it. We don't do this to shun society. We don't do this to buck laws. We certainly don't do this to get rich. We do this because we do not believe that the commercial alternatives are necessarily our best choice, and we believe that we can do better. And, based on public opinion (repeat sales), we do.

Those of us who are small producers don't consider that we are going to make much of an impact in the marketplace. All in all our products make up only a small percentage of the market. And I don't think any of us have the goal to price our products lower than the grocery store on these commodity items. What we offer is a unique product, direct from the source. The success of small farms in the local marketplace shows that some of the people of our state DO care about quality, sustainability, and other aspects that custom producers provide. All we ask is that our voice be heard even though we have no representation on the review committee.

The Michigan Right to Farm Act addresses commercial farm operations and it should apply equally to all commercial farms regardless of size or location. I am proud to be among those who have gone through our state court system to prove that the Michigan Right to Farm Act is a viable and valuable law for commercial farming operations. Michigan has a strong farming tradition and this tradition should be upheld, not only for major commercial producers, but also for promoters of genetic biodiversity, drug free living for our food products, and participation in our food production chain as small family farmers have done for centuries.

Vikki Papesh

{93}

Please reconsider the proposed changes to the Right to Farm Act, as it allows for and protects the rights of small local farms to provide their families and communities with local, sustainable/healthy food options & creates sustainability in food systems. Subjecting community farms to local zoning ordinances will severely limit or preclude farming activities in local areas, which is exactly what the Michigan Right to Farm Act set out to avoid. Local farm markets and our local economies will be negatively affected.

Please protect the Michigan Right to Farm act, so that small farms can rely on it knowing that they can carry out farming activities responsibly in the State of Michigan.

Rebecca Penney

{94}

Please do not support language against small backyard homestead families and put them out of "business". I am an early generation "Boomer" and learned how to supplement my family food (thank goodness). I am disgusted at what big Ag companies are allowed to do to the food that is "mass" consumed. GAAMPS should have language to support ALL safe agriculture practices, large and small. it should not be in the business of limiting people supporting their family with small businesses.

Candace Pilarski

{95}

I am a resident of Kalamazoo Township and have 5 chickens in a coop in my backyard. I would like to ask the committee to refrain from making changes that would make my owning and raising chickens where I live illegal. My friend David Hunter has been in the news a great deal lately reference his hobby farm. Although I don't intend to keep as many animals on my one acre as David has on his small farm, I would like to encourage your Taskforce not to make changes to Michigan rules that will restrict small farms and hobby farms and people like me from owning the animals that we currently have the right to own.

Catherine Pinto

{96}

Everyone in MI has a right to farm. Please don't restrict livestock in residential areas further.

Grace Potts

{97}

With increasing concerns with food safety I feel it is my right to provide food for my family by utilizing my private property. I am a so called "hobby" farmer who raises poultry for meat and eggs. I have 2 acres in Homer Township and feel like changes to this law would ban me from farming. Therefore I do not support changes to this law.

Michael Pressler

{98}

As you know Michigan's Right to Farm Act is the strongest in the country, and as currently written protects all farms that are compliant with applicable GAAMPs.

However, the proposed changes to the Site Selection GAAMP would weaken the Right to Farm protections for many small farms, potentially crippling local rood systems across the state.

Local food systems are the way of the future. In fact, had there not been a Local Food Summit scheduled on the same day as your meeting this week, I might have come to you in person.

Here, by the way, are a few of the topics the Local Food Summit will address, which would seem to underscore the importance of strengthening opportunities for local farming rather than preventing them:

- Understanding Community Food Systems
- Local Food Panel Discussions
- Overcoming Barriers and Results

Changes to the Site Selection GAAMP will inhibit the need to provide locally grown food for all Michigan communities — a goal I would imagine you as farmers would support.

I encourage MDARD members to support – not deter – farming operations in Michigan and to help farms of all sizes by not making changes to the Site Selection GAAMP.

Mike Riestererj

{99}

I see no need to change the GAAMPs, particularly for Manure Management and Utilization, Care of Farm Animals, Site Selection and Odor Control for New & Expanding Livestock Production Facilities, and Irrigation Water Use. There are already enough noise/nuisance/etc. ordinances that local governments can enforce that mean urban and sub-urban agriculture cannot get out of hand.

The shift in our society back to urban and sub-urban agriculture is a positive change in Michigan. As recently as WW2, our governments were encouraging such land usage. Now, we act as if in all of human history, cities have been devoid of commercial plant cultivation and animal husbandry. Preposterous!

Urban ag is phenomenally successful because city-dwellers relish local organic produce and poultry in particular.

As Detroit, Flint, and other Michigan cities try to re-invent themselves, urban ag has been a great help. Why handcuff their efforts? Let them grow! Leave the current situation in place and let our urban and sub-urban neighbors feed themselves and others.

Stu Roy

{100}

PLEASE protect the Michigan Right to Farm Act from changes that will affect the little guy. Please allow us to continue to have small family hobby farms, chicken coops or a goat or three without being over regulated by the government.

I want the right to feed my family food that I know the origins of. I want the right to Farm on the small scale protected. I want the right to strive to be self sufficient.

Gina Rubenstein

{101}

I live in Detroit where I operate an urban farm. The main product of the farm is duck eggs, and I currently keep 20 free range ducks in 4 city lots, and supply two restaurants with eggs, as well as a few private customers.

The farm has been a viable business in otherwise bleak times for the city, and it is one of the few good things that has come out the neighborhood's mass exodus. Not only does help the local economy, but we also hold fundraisers to fight blight, have an annual Easter party for the kids, and show many visitors some of the creative enterprises happening in the city. With 139 square miles of land in Detroit, there are plenty of opportunities to blend urban life with farm life. In fact, I get visitors from all over the country as well as Canada who come to the urban farms, as Detroit is considered the forefront of urban farming around the world. I am excited to see all the grassroots innovation from the citizens, as well as Michigan State University's recent involvement in Detroit's urban agriculture.

Officially, owning livestock has been illegal in Detroit. Unofficially, there is a moratorium on prosecuting urban farmers until the city comes up with their own guidelines for urban agriculture. But from what I hear, with a few exceptions, most people running the city have no idea what goes on in urban farms or small hobby farms. They wonder what happens with "all the duck sewage" that comes out of my property (currently they have 400 square feet per duck, so there isn't any duck sewage).

They have a myriad of other concerns, such as pesticide use, etc., that shows their total ignorance of the purpose of small farms. Jim Johnson, who is behind these new GAAMPs, also shows total ignorance when arguing these new proposals. For instance, 4999 chickens in someone's backyard is something that simply doesn't happen, and I don't think Johnson can come up with one example in real life that even comes close to that. Detroit may be founded on its factories, but factory farming has not taken root here.

Most urban farms and hobby farms are revolutionizing the way farming has been done over recent decades, and they are returning to organic practices, as well as more humane ways of raising livestock, which usually means fewer animals over a larger space. There is a market for this local food as more people choose to eat organically grown products and animal products from humane sources.

These proposed changes in the GAAMPs would not only limit consumers' choices at the checkout, but they would discourage small farms, and therefore small businesses, which are becoming a burgeoning industry in the state, as well as limiting our individual freedoms and restricting our property rights. I find it ironic that we are allowed to "stand our ground" when it comes to fighting crime, but the trend is to not allow us to "stand our ground" when it comes to the freedom to produce food in a safe and humane manner on our very own property. This, in my opinion, should be an inalienable right.

To tell people to move further into the country is not necessarily the answer either. Most farms, regardless of size, usually rely on another source of income, and these jobs usually require people to be near urban areas. Also, the customers that keep these farms viable live in the urban and suburban parts of the state. Requiring people to reside further on the outskirts would, for all intents and purposes, kill small farms. I know it is up to the individual municipalities to create their own laws regarding agriculture, but knowing that the laws could change, or that one's agricultural property could be zoned residential without warning would discourage people from investing in urban or suburban areas in the first place.

I rely on the Right To Farm Act to protect my business and my way of life in Detroit. It is the one foothold in an otherwise slippery slope of ignorance and corporate control of agriculture, and one of the many reasons I am proud to live in Michigan, and extremely honored to be part of the reinvention of Detroit. I propose that no changes be made to the GAAMPs until local governments are up to speed on some of the great things that are happening in urban agriculture and small farms in Michigan. Thanks for hearing me out, and please visit your local farm!

Suzanne Scoville

{102}

I urge you to not eliminate the loophole as described in the mlive article for small urban farmers. I want to know that when I eat animal products such as eggs that the chickens were not injected with hormones and not mistreated. Being a college student with no car I must live in an urban setting and my 3 chickens provide me with the protein I need to have a balanced diet to maintain my active lifestyle and the comfort in knowing exactly what I am consuming. My chickens are also heritage breeds and most farmers who sell eggs do not have farms with biodiversity of chicken breeds. Small backyard farmers like me ensure sustaining populations of these rare, dying out animal breeds.

Dean Simionescu

{103}

It is my understanding that the GAAMPs were created to help the farmer, big and small with maintaining the environment in a healthy way. The proposed changes have little or nothing to do with this. It seems to me that by prohibiting any farm activities in a residential area illegal, regardless of the amount of land owned could easily wipe out many farms as land is sold and more homes built. Re-zoning is not voted on but decided by those in charge of collecting more taxes (residential receiving more than ag). The RTFA should not have its teeth removed. The proposed action by the GAAMPS commission is illegal in that they have no authority to allow zoning to regulate Livestock facilities.

Mary Simpson

{104}

I am absolutely opposed to prospective changes proposed by GAAMP that would make illegal any livestock on land zoned for residential use only. I am concerned about the impact this change would have on local food security and on sustainable food systems especially on those of low or fixed incomes. Livestock, be it chickens or goats, rabbits or quail, worms (vermicomposting) or cod (aquaculture) produce economical animal products for low or fixed income families, and contribute to nutrient cycling for small gardening efforts. Additionally, and this bears underlining: these animals have the same minor nuisance risk as dogs or cats. The law must be applied consistently, or not at all. While it is possible to be irresponsible with livestock at any scale, make illegal the irresponsible care-taking of these animals, and let those responsible families utilize them as we in residential communities of all densities, have done for centuries.

Christian Smith

{105}

Please do not agree to restrict farm animals or farming in urban areas. Small farms and family farming is a right. We have the right to feed ourselves. I lament the lack of GMO free food in our grocery stores and reserve the right to grow my own.

Pamela Smithbell

{106}

I would like to let you know how important the right to farm protection is for small farmers, in times like these where food is very expensive and many people have allergies to processed foods it is vital that we be able to grow and raise our own food. I suffered from multiple illnesses before I found that I needed to drink goat milk instead of cow, and that I cannot tolerate processed food. As a nurse I barely make enough money to pay my bills, so getting a milk goat and a couple of chickens, and having my own garden enabled me to be healthy and to raise my kids healthy. The right to farm act saved me from the harassment of a neighbor, and enabled me to continue until I could afford to buy a little farm out in the country. It should be the right of every American to raise their own food, and the right to farm act should continue to protect small farmers.

Pam S. Smyth

•

{107}

The news of the proposed changes has reached far and wide – even to Minnesota. I would just like to point out that these changes will call a halt to food security.

The way to increase food security is to have many small, local producers. Thus if supply chains are bombed, or mega-farms destroyed, there is still food for the populace. Surely it is obvious that extending these rules to small farms (under 50 animals) will make it harder to farm and reduce the number of small farms, thus diminishing food security.

In addition, the rule plans to completely exclude livestock from residential neighborhoods. In a crisis, the neighbor with a few chickens will be an invaluable source of food security.

Perhaps you think there will never be a terrorist attack in the U.S. There could be a severe weather event – that might be harder to disbelieve – or an oil spill or a transportation shutdown for any of myriad causes.

Please do not pass these rules. Replace them with rules that make small farms easier!

Rev. Janet Spring

{108}

I am a small scale beekeeper in Jackson and I strongly urge you to reconsider your stance on altering the MDA's GAAMPS because small time farmers need protection to pursue farming that is not solely for the purpose of commercial, mass agriculture. My husband and I own one of Michigan's largest alternative beekeeping businesses and we simply would not exist if it weren't for the RTFA. Without it we surely would have left the state and taken our business and services elsewhere. Please do not make a decision that will force me to regret staying in my home state. These laws and guidelines cannot exclusively help the "big guys" you need to do more to listen to and act upon the wishes of the majority of your constituents.

Jessica Steller

{109}

Hello, I am writing as a concerned citizen. I believe that we need to legislate homeowners and their livestock less, not more. People have lived with livestock since we left the trees and became civilized. Livestock act as garbage disposals (kitchen wastes/scraps), food source, and health care providers (nutrient and minerals).

It is very concerning that we as a society continue to create barriers to citizens right to pursuit of happiness and liberty. People's rights should be upheld for all but the most dangerous actions, and living in health with livestock is not one of them. In fact, as a small amount of research shows, corporate ag. and confinement farming are BY FAR more dangerous pursuits, than individuals tending a small flock, hive, etc. Yet we allow leach fields, loss of topsoil, and animal cruelty routinely.

Please do not add the "Category 4 Sites" to the existing GAAMP's. This only hurts liberty. People should be rewarded for taking more responsibility in how they feed themselves, not further legislated. The time for rebellion is near, with economic stagnation, energy peaks, and the 1% getting richer by the day, the People are rumbling, it is your responsibility to listen.

Jesse D. Tack

{110}

I am writing to express my support for the Right to Farm. One of the most productive and positive movements currently is the farming movement in Detroit. As a resident, I have seen many vacant lots transformed into beautiful small farms. These farms serve the community in several ways:

1. They provide a source of healthy food
2. They engage the entire community in a positive community building activity
3. They beautify otherwise ugly and desolate spaces
4. They teach young people about the land and the environment.

Deborah Thompson

{111}

Please do not infringe on the rights of individuals to produce their own food, as currently protected under the Michigan Right To Farm Act.

Countless cities in the US, Canada, and Europe have demonstrated how urban and suburban farming can be successfully implemented to the satisfaction of both farmers and their neighbors. Americans who run small farms are regularly reduced to abandoning their livelihood in response to uneducated or petty complaints. We need to protect this most American of vocations.

Jessica Thompson,
who has fond hopes of having backyard chickens someday

{112}

As a suburbanite in the Detroit area in these changing times, I would ask that nothing be changed in Michigan law making it more difficult for urban and suburban citizens to raise farm animals on a small scale. I know of at least 6 families that raise chickens, for example, in several west side cities and Detroit and have never heard of their neighbors complaining. In Detroit, urban agriculture could be a piece of everyone's goal of improved conditions—it does not need any further hindrance! Please, please, do not let the state define any areas as off limits to small farm animals!

Virginia Thompson

{113}

I am writing to you to support the "Right to Farm" protection. Everyone should be allowed to raise their own chickens, etc. as long as guidelines are followed and the animals are well kept. Everyone should continue to have the right to be self sufficient, especially in this day and age where the economy has crashed for so many. Also, by raising your own animals, you can be certain of what they are fed and their overall health. For instance, I prefer to buy my eggs from a small farmer who feeds their chickens organic food as well as allows them to roam freely as this produces a healthier egg! I like to be able to visit the animals and see for myself how they are raised.

I also come from generations of families who did their own gardening and raised their own chickens. This is our "right" if we should choose to do so and I am adamantly against that right being taken away. Taking those rights away reflects a huge loss of freedom and is wrong on every level.

Anna Tomacari

{114}

I am writing you today concerned with the proposed changes to the Michigan Right to Farm Act. I believe it is the unalienable right of every citizen in this country and every resident of this state to grow their own food and raise their own livestock to be self sufficient, and an individuals personal rights and property rights should not be stripped away because a neighbor or government official does not like and/or agree with the farming they are doing. I do believe that reasonable restrictions can be placed on the number of animals being raised in conjunction with the size of the property to eliminate the potential for poor animal habitat and conflicts with neighbors, so long as those restrictions do not impede upon that individual's right to be self sufficient. Stripping a person of their rights because of social, political, or economical pressure is egregious.

It is my right to keep enough meat and egg chickens to sustain my nutritional needs as well as plant every square inch of that property in a garden if I so choose regardless of what any government official or government employee has to say about it. It is also my responsibility to ensure the animals have proper habitat and nutrition as well as my responsibility to control pest in the gardened areas of my property.

I urge you to drop all of the proposed changes to the Michigan right to farm act regarding small farms. We deserve to have our rights protected and for the current state law to protect us from our over infringing local governments. The fact that we need government to protect us from government is a joke in itself. If this infringement moves forward we will vote with our money and our feet.

JW

{115}

I am writing to express my OBJECTION to the proposed changes to Michigan's Right to Farm Act. It is important to me that all citizens in Michigan have a right to participate in the production of their own food, wherever they live.

I trust that justice will be served in this matter. Preserve Michigan's Right to Farm Act!

Lee Walsh

{116}

I am writing to express my concern over discussions being had to amend any part of the Michigan Right To Farm Act as it stands written. I have read both sides of the argument and it seems that politicians supporting such changes must be getting pressure from big agriculture or other special interests groups. Allowing people to grow their own food, even in residential zoned areas should not be frowned upon, it should be highly encouraged. Michigan has farming roots and a history of providing excellent food for our state and this Nation. In a time when Michigan needs more small business owners and entrepreneurial enterprises, why would you support shutting down small scale, local food production?

Ironically, many of the politicians I have spoke with can only site their personal experiences of large farming operations and claim that for the basis of further trying to limit the Right to Farm Act as it stands. If anyone in a residential zoned community decided to open a confinement hog operation, then obviously there should be something that prevents this...if their own common sense did not. However, if someone in a residential neighborhood wanted to have a small flock of backyard chickens, in a small moveable (by hand) chicken tractor, then why should they not have that option? Why is it that small scale food production in residential areas almost becomes criminal?

I am a teacher in Grand Haven and operate a small family farm on 7 acres of property zoned rural residential. We are currently protected by the Michigan Right To Farm Act, although not supported by current zoning laws. We have met with our township officials and I have been shocked to realize what little research they have done on small scale farming and what conclusions they have formulated based on their limited experience and research. I shared this with my high schools students as a way NOT to conduct business. It is embarrassing to watch our local leadership and now our state leadership make a case for shutting down small scale, local food production without any real good reason.

How is it that our state leadership feels they have the right to re-write something that has been part of our state for so long and what benefits will we see as a result of it? Will it strengthen communities and make them more self reliant? Will it help small business owners looking for local foods to serve in their restaurants? Does it help families trying to teach hard work and responsibility through food production? Any change to the current Michigan Right to Farm Act is wrong. I hope you receive many letters like this and a strong showing at the public meeting Wednesday. I will be sure to share this with my high school students and lead a discussion as to why our leaders in Lansing are trying to stop families for producing their own food. These students are smart and will figure it out pretty quick.... just follow the money is what they will say. Not sure how any of our leaders that support this sleep at night, knowing they are wrong.

Derek Warner

{117}

There are some things I like our government to be involved in and there are other things where they need to mind their own business. This is one of them. If somebody wants to have a little farm with chickens and other animals that can provide fresh, organic meat or dairy and they are in a so called city then for God's sake leave them alone and let them have their little farm.

Paul Webb

{118}

I am writing you today to express my concern over possible changes to the Michigan Right to Farm Act. I strongly believe that a "one size fits all" agricultural regulation is a bad fit for local food production in Michigan. One that is struggling economically.

Due to increasing costs and scarcity of pure, healthy food (no GMOs, hormones, pesticides, processing, additives, nutrient poor soil, etc.) my wife and I decided to supplement our food by growing some vegetables and raising a small flock chickens for eggs. We've been doing this for several years now and it's been very successful. Our neighbors approve and in addition we've been able to offset the maintenance costs through the sale of surplus eggs.

I believe it is everyone's right to provide for themselves and that includes owning a garden, having a small flock of chickens, or owning bees. Allowing and even encouraging these types of practices in communities enriches them, increases health of the people, educates and brings a level of awareness and responsibility to provide for oneself.

I understand concern about adding animals to urban areas, however by what standards are people owning other animals in urban areas considered acceptable? Cats kill local songbirds and get into fights with other cats and dogs. Dogs put adults and children and other animals at risk, wandering off onto other peoples' property as well as leaving their waste on the ground. Dogs commonly howl, bark and cause numerous disturbances at all hours of the day.

If these types of behaviors are acceptable and manageable in urban areas (which they are) then having a small flock of chickens, or a garden of tomatoes in no way poses a risk or hazard to citizens. Simply put, people have the right to grow their own food.

Scott White

{119}

I'm very upset to hear that there is being considered an across-the-board restriction on urban farming regarding keeping of animals by people in residential zones in Michigan. There are an incredible number of reasons that this trend is part of revitalizing our health, our economy, and our sustainability. Taking away this freedom is absolutely unacceptable. If there exist concerns about disease or other issues, they need to be directly addressed rather than having any sort of all-out prohibition. Concerns by some people about the mere appearance or symbolism of supposedly "farm" animals in urban settings have no place being considered as the freedom to keep animals is a far more important freedom than the freedom not to see them. If there are concerns about smell or other nuisances, that can be addressed directly. For the record, I do not myself have any farm animals, but I care deeply about this right and will work to oppose anyone trying to remove it.

Aaron Wolf

{120}

I am a suburban gardener who is informed about Michigan's Right to Farm Act. I am very opposed to the changes in GAAMPs. I'm not aware of the source of the inspiration for this change, but can only imagine it is highly political, as local townships (like my own in West Bloomfield) keep asserting their uninformed opinions and try to undermine the Right to Farm Act itself. As I keep explaining to any official that will listen, state law trumps local ordinances.

According to the law changes should be based on SCIENTIFIC EVIDENCE. What new evidence supports the current change to the site selection GAAMP?

According to the law, changes in the GAAMPs should be for the purposes of improved public health or environment. Residential zoned areas are not a threat to public health, nor the environment. In fact, if you look around other urban areas, you'll note that more and more small farms are growing their own food. If a person who lives in a residential area wishes to raise chickens, for example, they are subject to inspections to ensure that the site is clean and well maintained.

The Agriculture Commission has the authority to change the language of the GAAMPs, they do NOT have the authority to change the meaning of the law. Only legislators can do that!! It is time for Michigan's agricultural committees to stop overstepping the boundaries of the law. This will clearly have a huge fight if you decide to move forward. Food rights are a big topic right now and our citizens are dissatisfied with the state's hired hands overstepping the limits of their jobs to politically influence our lives.

Jennifer Yanover

{121}

With the preface of the Site Selection and Odor Control GAAMP is a statement that purports to "provide uniform, statewide standards and acceptable management practices based on sound science".

So with this in mind I would like to know what the sound science is that describes the new Category 4 and how exactly local zoning falls within statewide standards. Can the committee provide any citations that zoning is actually a true scientific based discipline? In fact, none of the proposed changes provide citations supporting the arbitrary changes. What is the real reason for the inclusion of Category 4? The wording, combined with the other proposed changes seem to be specifically aimed at excluding all Michigan citizens who happen to live in an area which has been arbitrarily labeled as residential.

The problem with "residential zone" is that it is anything that a local zoning board wants it to be. It has little to do with highly populated areas or land use. Local municipalities assign a residential zone to any household that they want to charge a higher tax base to. There is little rhyme and reason for some designations. It is certainly not scientific. Zoning changes are often changes to recoup taxes on devalued properties when city revenues are reduced.

My city, Garden City saw this in a wholesale zoning change from RF1 (resident farm, 1 family house) to Rl (1 family residence). So when I was cited for keeping livestock (chickens and honey bees) I attempted to use PA93 of 1981, The Right to Farm Act. With the proposed changes to this GAAMP, the opportunity to use that same State Law will be denied to me and any other Michigan citizen simply because of a mis-guided Category 4.

Furthermore, current farm operations in a Category 3 situation will also lose their rights if the "proximity" to Residential zones is added. If a new house is constructed and zoned as residential, the existing farm will be denied RTF protection. And that would be solely determined at the local level. Essentially, these changes are permitting a local government to decide who is afforded State-given Rights. These proposed changes violate the letter of the state law:

(6) Beginning June 1, 2000, except as otherwise provided in this section, it is the express legislative intent that this act preempt any local ordinance, regulation, or resolution that purports to extend or revise In any manner the provisions of this act or generally accepted agricultural and management practices developed under this act. Except as otherwise provided in this section, a local unit of government shall not enact, maintain, or enforce an ordinance, regulation, or resolution that conflicts in any manner with this act or generally accepted agricultural and management practices developed under this act.

I would like to point out that there were similar changes proposed for 2012 which were rejected by the Agriculture Commissioners. There is no reason for these proposed changes to be approved either. These changes, if approved, would be a serious economic blow to the citizens of Michigan. Freedom to raise one's own food, market and sell at farmer's markets would be eliminated. The chaos of each city or town enacting ordinances to protect animals, the environment and neighbors will result in legal challenges at every court level. There are no benefits to approving these changes. There will be severe consequences suffered state-wide if the changes are approved. In the end, this proposed change is detrimental to the health of the state economy and sovereign rights of the citizens of Michigan.

I urge you to reject this change. And if the other GAAMP proposed changes are as ill-conceived as this one, then they all should be rejected and returned to committee for a "sound science" evaluation.

Randy Zeilinger

EPILOGUE

This response of a thousand or more Michigan citizens was enough to delay a vote of the by a month, but on April 28, 2014, the Commission of Agriculture and Rural Development again approved changes to the GAAMPs that are impossible to meet, and appear to be designed to deny Right to Farm protection to the majority of Michigan citizens who live in areas that are "primarily residential" and are zoned residential[10]. Since then, a few local governments in Michigan have changed local ordinances to be more permissive, but many others have taken action against small farms in both urban and rural areas.

On November 12, 2014, the Draft GAAMPs for 2015 were presented to the Commission of Agriculture and Rural Development. Included in the Care of Farm Animal GAAMP are proposed changes that would make it significantly more difficult to keep bees in both urban and rural areas, by requiring that 6 foot high solid fences be constructed between the hive and any property line that lies within 200 feet of the hive[11].

---

10 April 28, 2014 Minutes of the Michigan Commission of Agriculture and Rural Development
11 November 12, 2014 Minutes of the Michigan Commission of Agriculture and Rural Development

ACKNOWLEDGEMENTS

The cover photo was taken by Andy Dragt in September 2012, on Wealthy Street in Grand Rapids, Michigan. Used with permission.

Book design and layout by Lee Lewis Walsh at http://www.wordsplusdesign.com.

RESOURCES

http://www.michigansmallfarmcouncil.org

https://www.facebook.com/michigansmallfarmcouncil

http://sustainablefarmpolicy.org

www.ingramcontent.com/pod-product-compliance
Lightning Source LLC
Chambersburg PA
CBHW021830020426
42334CB00014B/570